MW00636648

Race and the Cosmos

Barbara A. Holmes

RACE

AND THE

COSMOS

An Invitation to View the World Differently

Barbara A. Holmes

CAC PUBLISHING
Center for Action and Contemplation
cac.org

Race and the Cosmos
Copyright © 2002, 2020 by Barbara A. Holmes

All rights reserved. No part of this book may be reproduced, stored in a retrieval system, or transmitted, in any form or by any means, electronic, mechanical, photo-copying, recording, or otherwise, without the written permission of the publisher.

"My Grandfather Was a Quantum Physicist," copyright © 1983 by Duane Big Eagle, published in *Songs from This Earth on Turtle's Back: Contemporary American Indian Poetry*, ed. Joseph Bruchac (Greenfield Center, NY: Greenfield Review Press, 1983) was reprinted by permission, 2002.

Requests for information should be addressed to:
CAC Publishing
PO Box 12464
Albuquerque, NM 87195

Cover design: Nicholas Kramer with Cliff Berrien
Interior design: Nelson Kane

Library of Congress Cataloging-in-Publication Data

Holmes, Barbara Ann,
      Race and the cosmos: an invitation to view the world differently /
      Barbara A. Holmes.
        p. cm.
      Includes bibliographical references.
      ISBN 1-56338-377-2 (2002)
      ISBN: 978-1-62305-050-4 (2020)
      1. African American—Religion. 2. Race—Religious aspects—Christianity.
      3. Religion and science. 4. Cosmology.

      Printed in the United States of America

To much-loved sons:
Jason Stokes – for the spirit and joy in your music
Marcus Stokes – for the insight and creativity in your films

The Spirit whispers,
the ancestors agree.
You are star born
and God loved;
The universe awaits
your gifts.

:::

This universe is not a tragic expression of meaningless chaos but a marvelous display of orderly cosmos.

—Martin Luther King, Jr.,
Strength to Love

:::

When midwives in the slave quarters delivered a child, they always looked to see if the child was born with a veil of membrane over its face. Being born with the gossamer veil was a sure sign that the child's vision would reach to the heavens. Barefaced tots had flat-world eyes that screeched to a halt at apparent edges, but not the veiled ones. Behind those lids would scroll the cosmic visions of worlds unseen, and quantum dreams of wriggling, resonating, infinitesimal things.

—Barbara A. Holmes

:::

God is hiding in the world.
Our task is to let the divine emerge from our deeds.

—Rabbi Abraham Heschel,
I Asked for Wonder: A Spiritual Anthology

:::

Every one of us is, in the cosmic perspective, precious. If a human disagrees with you, let him [or her] live. In a hundred billion galaxies, you will not find another.

—Carl Sagan,
Cosmos

:::

:::

Contents

:::

Acknowledgments

2020

I WROTE THIS BOOK because of my fascination with the mysteries of the life journey, the whispers of the elders, and the beckoning of night skies. When it was first published in 2002, I was teaching seminary students in Memphis, Tennessee. Once again, I was living in the Deep South, in a bustling city with a haunted history.

It was in this place, where Elvis Presley gyrated, Martin Luther King, Jr. was killed, and Ida B. Wells-Barnett challenged the lynching culture, that my fatigue and angst about issues of "race" in America aligned with my fascination with cosmology. This second edition explores race and the rhetoric of cosmology during current times.

The acknowledgments from the first edition (below) name the people, places, and organizations that guided me on this journey of rhetorical discovery. Eighteen years later, I remain grateful for their support, and for the contributions of new friends. I am grateful to Kirsten Oates for her insightful guidance of this project, to the Center for Action and Contemplation for its inspired educational contributions that help us to see the world differently, to Fr. Richard Rohr for his spiritual leadership and cosmic worldview, and to Cliff Berrien for his wisdom, conference collaborations, and interest in my work. Danielle Isabelle Berrien made this second edition possible. My gratitude for her labor of love with the manuscript knows no bounds. Finally, I am grateful to Vanessa Guerin and Shirin McArthur for their editorial insights and Nicholas Kramer for his creative collaboration with Cliff Berrien and Gigi Ross.

Now and always, I am grateful for a life filled with wonder, for the love of my husband, George Edward Ford, and for occasional glimpses of glory in an unfolding universe.

2002

I AM THE GRATEFUL recipient of a 2001 syllabus grant award from the John Templeton Foundation in conjunction with Center for Theology and the Natural Sciences at the Graduate Theological Union in Berkeley, California, which was given to explore this topic in the classroom. Physicist Johnny Holmes and astronomer Br. Kevin Ryan of Christian Brothers University in Memphis, Tennessee, inspired me, answered my questions, and lectured in my Science and Liberation Theology course. Although I am especially indebted to these men, any errors or misinterpretations of scientific theories are mine alone. I am inspired also by the work of Victor Anderson, Lewis V. Baldwin, Howard Harrod (1932–2003), and Marcia Y. Riggs.

I offer special thanks to the students in my Science and Liberation Theology class (2002), who engaged in stimulating discussions and innovative translations of the discourses of science, culture, and religion. I appreciate the participation of John Kaplan, Wyvonia Harris, Jerry Hastings, Elizabeth Lindsey, Nancy Dekar, Arkotong Longkumer, Ryan Boatright, Sharon Gazaway, Darren Kennemer, Murphy Helms, Tom Martin, Lynne Sharman, and Stephen Wiseman.

My appreciation of issues of cosmology and difference in Native American, African, Hispanic, and Asian contexts was enhanced by conversations with Tim Tseng, West African scholar Marcel Oyono, Luis Pedraja, and scholars and denominational leaders of the Choctaw Nation Virginia Espinoza and Randy James. My friend Karen Jenkins, past president of Brethren Colleges Abroad, encouraged my focus on global issues, Pam Chavis elicited my poetic side, and my mother, Mildred Holmes, supported and encouraged yet another leap of faith.

My sister the Honorable Susan Holmes challenged me to probe the possibilities. My sister and educator Eileen Clay reminded me that the children of the next generation are the real audience for this work, and sister Mildred Williams, MSW, kept me abreast of the social and mental health crises that decades of oppression spawn. To Janet and Thomas Holmes, you are loved and appreciated.

:::

Preface to the Second Edition

Let us all hope that the dark clouds of racial prejudice will soon pass away and the deep fog of misunderstanding will be lifted from our fear-drenched communities, and in some not too distant tomorrow the radiant stars of love and [sisterhood and] brotherhood will shine over our great nation with all their scintillating beauty.
—Martin Luther King, Jr., "Letter from a Birmingham Jail"

SO MUCH HAS CHANGED since Dr. King expressed his hope for a "not too distant tomorrow" of radiant human mutuality. Decades later, issues of race and racism remain as problematic as ever. The more things change, the more they stay the same. Changes in the study of cosmology reflect our growing knowledge about the universe, its origins, and its functioning. Many of the scientific theories that I relied upon for my analysis have changed since this book was first published in 2002.

However, the clouds of race and racism in America continue to loom, threatening and dangerous. Moreover, in 2020, the ghosts of oppression are shape-shifting into new forms and expanding their territory. Despite the apparent advances of women, people of color (POC),[1] and the

1. POC refers to people of color. It has recently been updated to BIPOC in order to interject specificity into identification of oppression. "B" stands for black and "I" for

LGBTQIA+ community, racism, violence, xenophobia, and anti-immigrant tropes seem to be on the rise.

Although this is a discouraging reality, I am convinced that a community-called-beloved is possible. This is an admittedly fragile possibility, but it is not a utopian dream. I believe that people of good will harbor a persistent hope that our planet can be a place of belonging for all its inhabitants. To view the world differently is to recognize the delusions that we have willingly embraced and admit our own complicity in the empowerment of systems of oppression.

In America, we have encoded the languages of equality, freedom, and justice into our myths of national "goodness," yet we remain infatuated with power and privilege. Also, we support corrupt and rapacious political and economic systems that prey on the vulnerable. It will take a shift in language and purpose to free us from this limited and materialistic view of human potential.

Perhaps the languages of science, cosmology, and physics can help us to see our plight and our opportunity. We know that the sciences offer no magic solutions, but something must be done! Divisive elements in society have become emboldened. Recently, it was reported that the office of the Highlander School, a training site for nonviolent activism during the Civil Rights era, was burned, destroying some irreplaceable documents.

A few weeks later, the world saw the silhouette of a black hole for the first time and fires (of unknown origin) "broke out" in three black churches in Louisiana, the Cathedral of Notre Dame in Paris, and Jerusalem's Al-Aqsa Mosque, Islam's third holiest site. I am reminded of a couplet in the spiritual, *Oh Mary Don't You Weep:* "God gave Noah the rainbow sign / No more water, the fire next time."[2]

With sacred buildings burning and chaos in our social systems, we are in such dire need of vision, imagination, and love of neighbor that this rhetorical experiment is worth a try. Currently, we are using language to disguise our commonalities and exacerbate our differences. Narratives about POC often emphasize inherent inferiority and criminality, when

---

indigenous. Despite this suggested change, I will use POC as a general category that covers all persons of color.

2. Traditional spiritual, as quoted in James Baldwin, *The Fire Next Time* (New York: Vintage, 1993), 106.

the truth is that all of us embody stardust and a divine spark with cosmic origins.

We come from mystery and return to it at the end of the life journey. What a gift to be on earth during an era when the universe is making itself known to and through the human race. We are part of an unfolding that is ongoing, yet, around the planet, people and systems are in crisis and we don't seem to know what to do. Even if we had solutions, they could not be implemented fast enough to save lives. Perhaps the first steps require that we free ourselves from negative stereotypes and recognize our common cosmic origins.

Of course, I am aware that, to some folks, a book about using the languages of physics and cosmology to deconstruct racism may seem like magical thinking, like a game of Scrabble played in the path of an approaching tornado. I agree that the social situation is urgent, but frantic responses to resilient problems will not solve anything. I am not suggesting that we stargaze while families are separated and babies are caged at national borders, or that we contemplate the universe while our dark and beloved children catch bullets in their backs as they run from the police through city/suburban/anywhere streets.

Instead, I am suggesting that the languages of physics and cosmology offer powerful analogies that reveal our cosmic and spiritual identities and empower our collective creativity. One thing is certain: Although we cannot reason our way out of this quandary, we can allow the universe to reveal its secrets through us. We can contemplate and consider together. We can expand our spiritual and cosmic vocabulary and allow the mysteries of life to permeate every cell. We have waited long enough. It's time to take the transcendent leap forward in hopes of personal and communal healing as well as a shared cosmic future. This book offers one rhetorical pathway toward that end.

⁙

Preface to the First Edition

W ISE WOMEN AND MEN admit that life is a mystery. Scientific and religious probes confirm the premise. Certainly, there are facts, figures, concepts, and linkages of understanding that crisscross the vast, unknowable aspects of human life, but always there is mystery. Because this aspect of the life space is pervasive and unyielding, one wonders how we make the leap from horse and buggy to space shuttles, from inkwells to fax machines and digital imaging. In part, we bring that which we never knew into view through ideas, words, concepts, and analogies that enlighten and encourage us to inquire and take tentative steps toward new horizons of understanding.

This book seeks new vistas of understanding in the study of "race" by juxtaposing cultural and scientific ideas. Using the methodological lens of rhetorical analysis and the category of analogy, unlikely concepts taken from the study of race and cosmology are conjoined to suggest new approaches to the dilemma of difference. To be certain, this is an unusual thought experiment. The words "race" and "cosmos" are seldom used in the same sentence and seem to have little, if anything, to do with one another. However, I am suggesting that once familiar rhetorical categories are expanded beyond the political and social, everything may have everything to do with everything else.

This interdisciplinary study sheds light on issues that seem familiar but continue to confound us. The unhappy fact may be that we have assumed too much about our understanding of issues of difference and our knowledge of the cosmos. We thought that we had a grasp of race after the Civil Rights movement. It seemed so simple. Those who opposed equal rights and civil liberties seemed to be oppressors and evil manipulators of the life space. However, before we could settle into the smugness that certainty spawns, issues of race, gender, and class challenged each of us and made it impossible to assign, without qualifiers and explanations, the role of oppressor or victim.

For it is apparent that we cannot be reconciled to one another by using the language of oppression, victimization, and overcoming. We need new connections to universal and cosmic realities in order to divest oppressors of historical narrative advantages and to offer victims alternatives to entrenched and internalized narratives of violation.[1] For besieged minority and marginalized communities locked into discussions of power and victimization, scientific languages offer flashes of insight about race, identity, and the moral life within the broader context of the cosmos.

Race signifies the way in which we orient ourselves toward one another based on perceived categorical differences of color, culture, or ethnicity. The fact that race does not exist as a category of "human biological diversity" does not discount its effects.[2] The resilience of the idea is rooted in deeply sedimented cultural beliefs. Those beliefs are strengthened by the residual effects of scientific and social assessments of inferiority and by reductionist theological discourses that focus on the antithesis of darkness and light.

The idea of race is also perpetuated by racism. Martin Luther King, Jr. (1929–1968) defined racism as "the myth of an inferior race, of an inferior

1. See Kathryn Tanner's discussion of victim/oppressor modalities in *The Politics of God: Christian Theologies and Social Justice* (Minneapolis: Augsburg Fortress, 1992). See also William F. McDonald, *The Criminal Victimization of Immigrants,* Palgrave Studies in Victims and Victimology (Cham, Switzerland: Springer International, 2018).

2. C. Loring Brace, foreword to Ashley Montagu, *Man's Most Dangerous Myth: The Fallacy of Race,* 6th ed. (Walnut Creek, CA: AltaMira, 1997), 14. See also Robert Wald Sussman, *The Myth of Race: The Troubling Persistence of an Unscientific Idea* (Cambridge, MA: Harvard University Press, 2014).

people."[3] Audre Lorde (1934–1992) defined it as "the belief in the inherent superiority of one race over all others [sic] and thereby the right to dominance, manifest and implied."[4] Today we know that there are many ethnicities but only one race: the human race. While race may not have scientific origins, it cannot be relegated to the refuse pile until its very real offspring—"racism"—is no longer a hindrance to intercultural moral flourishing.[5]

Cosmology concerns itself with the origins and nature of the universe, within the rigorous contexts of physics and astronomy. However, cosmology is also a rhetorical signifier of human striving and creativity in the universe. Because the cosmos seems to be within our reach, it engages our imagination and is filtered through the matrix of human experience and interpretation. Because it is always beyond our reach, our cognitive and language appropriations cannot diminish its wonders and mysteries.

Try as we might, we cannot separate our ideas about the life space from our ideas about one another. In the past, commonly held beliefs about a mechanistic, cause-and-effect universe supported oppressive and hierarchical social practices. Emerging views of a cosmos that is characterized by holism, indeterminacy, and interconnections have the potential to empower people from the two-thirds world in ways that liberation theology has not.[6] As it turns out, liberation, its methods, and its goals are more complex than we imagined.

3. Everett Gendler, "Conversation with Martin Luther King," *Conservative Judaism* 22, no. 3 (Spring 1968), 16.

4. Audre Lorde, *Sister Outsider: Essays and Speeches* (Trumansburg, NY: Crossing Press, 1984), 124. Also, Audre Lorde, "The Uses of Anger: Women Responding to Racism," *Women's Studies Quarterly* 9, no. 3 (Fall 1981), https://academicworks.cuny.edu/wsq/509/.

5. In this book, the word "race" is treated as if it is in quotation marks even when it is not.

6. I am as perplexed as anyone as to the "proper" label for the part of the world that includes people of color and emerging Asian, Hispanic, and African nations. For those of us who specialize in global and intercultural studies, there are few consistent identifying labels for these emerging communities. Some refer to these communities as "first or third world." However, I find this designation confusing. I recognize that the re-appropriation of "first" language takes into account the primacy of indigenous cultures. However, it also encodes modernist leanings toward hierarchy. For the purposes of this book, I shall refer to the collective of nations and people from indigenous or ethnic origins as "the two-thirds world" to emphasize their majority status and intercultural connections.

Through telescopic space images and quantum mathematical formulas, we are being introduced to a vastly different view of our world. It is a view that has the potential to engender a freedom that comes in unexpected forms. I find freedom in a vibrating multidimensional string theory; in the powerful, cohesive, and mysterious substance of dark matter and dark energy; in the perplexing world of quantum mechanics; and in the mysteries of the big bang.

This newness is just within reach. This newness may not be newness at all. Instead, it may be an epoch of awareness, a tear in the veil that separates realities, and an opportunity to glimpse the potential seeded in us and in the cosmos. This newness may transform the self-understanding and life perspectives of marginalized people everywhere. It is a reasonable hope on a living planet in a universe that is responding and wondrous.

:::

Quantum physics is rich with imagery
that almost begs for application to the experiences of daily life.

—Danah Zohar,
The Quantum Self

:::

Each person lives in the center of the cosmos. . . .
The actual origin and birthplace is not a scientific idea;
the actual origin of the universe is where you live your life.

—Brian Swimme,
The Hidden Heart of the Cosmos

:::

:::

Introduction:

Treading New Ground

SITTING IN THE LOUNGE of the Faculty Club in Berkeley, California, at yet another conference on the issue of race, it occurred to me that I embody the discomfort that has marked the end of public dialogue about race and liberation in lived contexts. I have never experienced oppression in neat categories. Instead, as an African American woman, I have been bound and free, seriatim, simultaneously, and as an interjection when I least expected it. The intersecting modalities of race, sex, gender, and class create kaleidoscopes of possibility and limitation.

I come from an African people who lived in the midst of these intrinsic ambiguities. I am part South Carolinian Gullah/Geechee (on my father's side) and part West African of unknown national/tribal origin, from the densely populated slave camps on the Maryland eastern shore (on my mother's side). My father's people were short, stocky, rice-growing Bantu types and one or two lanky Cherokees who worked hard and died early. My mother's people included an eclectic mix of freckle-faced fair and dark-skinned folks with high foreheads, who worked field and house and lived well into their nineties. Since the first publication of this book, family members have tested their DNA, and we now know that the stories of our links to West Africa, Sierra Leone, and Ghana are predominant and correct. But our genetic lineage also includes lesser ties to Britain, Ireland, and Asia.

Throughout this history, narrative and genetic, I have not experienced life as a series of orderly or certain events, but as a kaleidoscope of experiences that evolve and recede. It has been a journey of faith from somewhere to somewhere else. Like others who have been encouraged to excel, "becoming" was the agenda, potential was the fuel, and the great liberation movements provided the context.

We can now admit in retrospect that Western cultures shared a profound naïveté about liberation. The path toward an egalitarian society seemed linear and goals were deemed to be determinate and reachable. Yet, deterministic models of freedom created mirages of confusion that lured the unwary. The idea of liberation as definitive "overcoming" enticed a generation with phantom promises of "progress."

Moreover, legal and social gains that secured basic human rights did not assuage the deeply sedimented angst of ethnic communities. Although many things changed for the better and we are freer than our ancestors in many respects, in other respects we are not.

This book suggests that liberation will not be found in utopian theological models, legal mandates, or social engineering projects. If the dialogue about race, identity, and the moral life is to be resurrected from the stylized jousting of weary opponents, it will need a language that includes clues about a complex universe that is wondrous and rife with uncertainty. This invitation to view the world differently is one that has been extended by God, prophets, philosophers, scientists, and wise women and men throughout the ages.[1]

I am suggesting that we view issues of race and liberation from the perspective of the cosmos, and that we begin to incorporate the languages of science into our discussions of liberation. This is a reasonable choice, given the reality that the universe is an integral aspect of any human

1. My use of invitational language is not new. Other theologians at the intersection of religion and science also use the language of invitation. To name two, Diarmuid O'Murchu, *Quantum Theology: Spiritual Implications of the New Physics* (New York: Crossroad, 2000) and Albert N. Wells, *The Christian Message in a Scientific Age* (Richmond, VA: John Knox, 1962) include this language in their books. Invitation is the language of covenant. In the language of Yeshua, the invitation is to become aware of multiple realities and God's engagement with the world.

endeavor, even when it is a taken-for-granted backdrop for our activities. I am challenging all justice seekers to awaken to the vibrant and mysterious worlds of quantum physics and cosmology. Recent discoveries on cosmic and quantum levels are as dramatic as the realization that the sun does not rotate around the earth. All of the narratives that frame reality have been unsettled by the Hubble telescope's unblinking eye and strangely responsive but unseen quantum elements. From cosmic and quantum realms we learn that we are connected to one another in unexpected ways. Theoretical physics suggests that, even when separated, entities that have once been in contact will react to changes in the other.

The truth is that our images of life in community changed when we realized that the world was not flat. Everything will change again when interhuman dominance is seen as a false construct in the universe. A level playing field is being offered to those who can grasp the concepts as tangible precursors of freedom. As amazing as it may seem, the physical sciences offer creative rhetorical tools that may help us to rethink the dynamics of race relations within the broader context of the cosmos.

Despite our best efforts, race remains a difficult issue in North America. Perhaps it's because our attractions and aversions to one another have seeped so deeply into the culture; perhaps it's because we did not have the cathartic benefits of a South African Truth and Reconciliation Commission after slavery. Whatever the cause, racial wounds continue to fester. Yet something has changed. Our public conversations about race have become ritualized. They are also completely unlinked from descriptions of the life space that emerge from the realms of physics and cosmology.

In an age of astounding scientific findings that allude to a world that is holistic, relational, and intrinsically diverse, most of us are conducting business as usual. We pay homage to fallen leaders of the liberation movements on the dates of their demise or birth, and we reminisce about valiant skirmishes for justice during the 1960s. Nostalgic strains of freedom songs loop in our collective memories as symbols of the struggles, optimism, and determination of the era. But the energy for liberation has dissipated and the impetus for justice has stalled.

Fifty years after the liberation movements exploded out of Latin and African American contexts, ethnic communities are still beset by devastating and intransigent economic, cultural, and racial forces. Something has gone awry. Many folks wonder whether liberation movements made a bad bargain when they exchanged the autonomy and self-reliance nurtured in closed communities for "rights" with shallow legal and social roots that continue to wither with each passing generation.

The intriguing factor is that while race is no longer the primary focus of public and private debate, it still keeps us tethered to its mythologies. We may murmur that such matters are in the past and that we need to get on with the business of life, but the immediacy of difference, fear, alienation, and hatred continually confronts us. No longer a closed discussion between blacks and whites, the move toward a beloved community of reconciled groups and individuals now encompasses the concerns of all marginalized communities.

As an African American, I have specific concerns about the well-being of my own community, but I am also acutely aware of the similar cries for justice from African, Native American, Asian, Hispanic, and indigenous communities throughout the world. Accordingly, although this book uses the African American community as a model for appropriating the new discourses emerging from physics and cosmology, it includes the voices of other communities. My hope is that this book will encourage all of us to explore and use science and its startling new options for discussing our own culturally specific issues.

When I speak of the African American community, or any other community for that matter, I do not presume that there is a single collective with agreed-upon purposes and goals. Although marginalized ethnic communities may develop ascertainable contours and shared narratives because of common causes, origins, and crises, they may not agree on methods or priorities. These disagreements are more likely to surface during times of safety but remain submerged during times of individual or communal siege.

I am aware, as I use the word "marginalized," that none of the buzzwords in racial discourse have lost their power. If you doubt that this is true, ask anyone in your circle of friends and family to respond to the words "victimization," "oppression," or "marginalization" within the context of race and ethnicity. Most will say that these words no longer accurately describe the status of race relations in the United States. Sometimes the names of prominent people of color will be used in support of the argument that things have changed. Realists, cultural theorists, and folks at the local barbershop and beauty parlor know better.

The names used to support the idea of racial advancement change more frequently than the reality. Yet, the questions persist. If things have progressed, if ostensible public advancements are evident in the African American community, why does the gap between perception and reality continue to widen? Why does the community-at-large seem to embody such a deep sense of loss tinged with hopelessness? The core issues seem to be related to a sense of alienation and nihilism that renders progress meaningless and nurtures a subliminal rage that is catabolic in its intensity.

There is also a lack of rootedness, a loss of primal connections to universal realities and a cosmic inability to lament or to mine the "race drama" consistently for its tragic/comedic and pedagogical elements. The ancestors possessed these abilities and used them in ways that we have long forgotten. They could laugh, even during calamity, and weep with abandon during the seasons for sorrow. This ability to take the full measure of life experiences helped to keep despair from overtaking them.

It is one thing to make these pervasive pronouncements about a mix of malaise and yearning that is endemic throughout the African American community as theory; it is quite another to see the immediate effects of loss and detachment in my own context. I recount one incident, not because it is exemplary of race-related issues, but simply to emphasize the sense of displacement and disconnection lurking just beneath the surface of ostensible progress. It is also offered to interject the need for cultural appropriations of scientific ideas.

I was teaching a course called African Religions in the Diaspora with Dr. Marcel Oyono, a West African colleague from Cameroon, when students began overriding the planned subjects of discussion to inquire about their own origins. They wanted to know if there was any way that Dr. Oyono could assess their body types or facial structures to connect them to a country or tribe on the African continent. Although the yearning was palpable, I was uncomfortable. Their requests reminded me of pseudo-sciences (like the bell curve) that reappear in every generation to label and assess inferiority and intelligence by physiognomy.[2]

2. Richard J. Herrnstein and Charles A. Murray, *The Bell Curve: Intelligence and Class Structure in American Life* (New York: Free Press, 1994). See also Claude S. Fischer

The students wanted Dr. Oyono to look at them and tell them that they were Bantu or Fon, Yoruba or Akan. Using language and cultural cues, he was quite skilled at discerning tribal connections among his African kin, but to ask him to peer back through the centuries to link a smile or jutting chin to ancestral origins seemed to be a bit too much. Here we were in the new millennium, and some of our graduate students were expressing a critical longing to belong. The consistently urgent requests for origins and connections continued in subsequent classes.

This was more than mere curiosity or historical nostalgia. Students suggested DNA testing as a possible option to reconnect the African diaspora with the motherland. Their suggestions were fueled by a story on the television show *60 Minutes* that connected the Lemba, a South African tribe, to their Jewish heritage. In this remarkable story, it was determined through genetic testing that years of indigenous narrative history about tribal Semitic origins were grounded in fact.

Students were certain that this story supported their theory that similar testing techniques might identify their own African origins. Although we explained the difficulties of such direct associations and testing, I am certain that we did not assuage the deep longings that emerged during this course.

Now, of course, we know those students were right. Today, DNA testing is part of Western cultural curiosity and several DNA testing companies can actually reconnect some people of African descent to their tribal origins.[3]

As for the students, my colleague and I did what we could at the time. We used the opportunity to talk about the origins and history of West African people and to describe the vast ethnic diversity on the continent and in the diaspora. When the class was over, my colleague thanked me for a good semester and gave me an African name. He called me Ezagon, "first loved daughter of my father." I had no illusions that this "naming" event would transport me beyond the "danger waters" of the Middle Passage

---

et al., *Inequality by Design: Cracking the Bell Curve Myth* (Princeton: Princeton University Press, 1996) and Michael E. Staub, *The Mismeasure of Minds: Debating Race and Intelligence between Brown and The Bell Curve* (Chapel Hill: University of North Carolina Press, 2018).

3. Historian Henry Louis Gates hosts a PBS television show that traces identity through DNA and historical records.

or reconnect me to mother Africa. As far as I was concerned, such connections were not necessary to my well-being. I intended to respond with reserved gratitude and instead was startled by the stammered yearning from my own lips. This African name was a wisp, a cloud—nothing really. Yet, it was everything.

This is not to say that naming rituals will address or assuage the subliminal but perpetual sense of loss many Africans in the diaspora live out daily. To the contrary, such rituals often foster false assumptions of connections and understanding that are usually peripheral at best. There are stories about Nelson Mandela (1918–2013) being greeted by African American audiences who festooned his lectern with Kente cloth and other West African artifacts. It was clear that those who wanted to welcome him had no understanding of space or place or the vastness of the African continent and the complexity and diversity of its cultures. I have certainly been guilty of similarly incongruous acts.

Upon Nelson Mandela's visit to Memphis, some of us felt the irrepressible and misguided need to let out a high-pitched screech that sounded more like a strangled chicken than the guttural South African vocalization that we were trying to mimic as a welcome. Mandela's polite but slightly bemused look spoke of the extent of his tolerance as he graciously accepted our bizarre vocalizations amid the applause. He must have known of our need to connect—by any means necessary. For African Americans, this need to connect to origins is seldom voiced; it is worn, breathed, and murmured in prayer. It is ached, and suffered, and then denied.

Where race is concerned, there are more questions than answers. Most discussions tend to be steeped in the myth of ostensible progress. The equal opportunity discomfort on all sides of the issue stems from the vast disjuncture between effort, desire, and outcome. At this point, the road to racial reconciliation appears to be endless, and we are weary travelers. The chapters in this book outline a proposed movement toward the rich, rhetorical resources that cosmology and quantum physics offer a multicultural society. By using analogical propositions, I can clarify unfamiliar or difficult concepts by linking the familiar with the unfamiliar, thereby shedding light on both.

Chapter 1 focuses on awareness and its consequences in rhetorical, personal, and collective contexts. To awaken means that we are subject to trauma, but also to healing. If that were not enough, it also means that we must maintain some level of sentient consciousness or, in the vernacular, "stay woke." We need to know who we are. We also need to know whether our choices and relationships are random and futile or tethered to a force that exceeds our conceptual limitations.

Chapter 2 examines the limitations of social, theological, and political descriptions of liberation. In the United States, there are agreed-upon and stabilizing narratives about self, nature, God, and society drawn from these disciplines. The lesson of postmodernity is that many of these narratives helped to maintain social and political hegemonies.

Moreover, the languages of science were missing and the view of liberation was limited. It would take a while to realize that people who have internalized the malignancies of racism need more than songs and chants to recover. New meanings and identifying metaphors had to be claimed. Chapter 3 examines the perils and possibilities of integrating the discourses of science and religion into the lives of ordinary people. This chapter introduces some key scientific concepts that will inform the discussion about culture and race. It also traces the historical interactions of science and religion.

Chapter 4 considers indigenous cosmologies and critiques of science. This chapter juxtaposes Western scientific discourses with the powerful concepts and metaphors about the universe drawn from ancestral wisdom. Chapter 5 engages issues of race and cosmology. The premise is that cosmological analogies offer new and empowering perspectives of self and society. For individuals and communities that have assimilated negative assumptions about their worth and potential, this is a crucial change. New questions arise when darkness becomes a metaphor for power and cosmic predominance. Theories of individual and communal responsibility must be revisited when human potential and limitations are not described as social constructions, but as quantum and cosmological legacies.

Chapter 6 engages the idea of dominance and quantum theory. In Western societies, previously dominant cultures are seeking ways to orient themselves toward difference without losing the sense of order and control that once stabilized a traditional life perspective. The concepts that emerge from recent findings in quantum physics emphasize uncertainty as an integral part of reality. Such findings will ultimately influence our perceptions of one another and the world.

Chapter 7 discusses the idea of a beloved community, a place of hope and moral fulfillment for those who have been deemed peripheral because of their gender, sexuality, or ethnicity. I am proposing the creation of a community that embraces science as well as theological, aspirational, and pragmatic contours. To distinguish the two descriptions of community, I have slightly altered the name. Here, it will be referred to as "a community-called-beloved"—a geo-spiritual space where people seek and do justice because they remember all of their connections: cosmic, social, and divine. Once they have worked out the particulars of egalitarianism, they name this voluntary and sometimes difficult association desirable, healing, and beloved.[4]

Chapter 8 discusses the search for meaning in a world that has suddenly shifted on its epistemological axis. Here, I explore the challenges and possibilities for socially marginalized persons who are reconnecting and identifying with emerging scientific narratives of holism.

It is perhaps late in this discussion to admit that I am not a scientist. I cannot claim to be more than a theologian/ethicist/activist and lawyer with serious scientific interests. This book is not an attempt to explain theoretical physics or cosmology. There are excellent texts that can provide that information. I am testing cultural concerns on the anvil of scientific languages that have the potential to illuminate the life experience and self-definition of the two-thirds world. The very nature of rhetorical analysis and moral discourse assumes that language can penetrate realms that remain off-limits because of disciplinary boundaries.

I mention this because, after the publication of the first edition, questions arose as to whether or not readers could rely on my scientific statements. That question can be answered very simply: All scientific statements are quoted or cited to experts in the field. The following quote

---

4. When I refer to the "beloved community," I am using the language of social and eschatological hope coined in the early days of the twentieth century by the philosopher-theologian Josiah Royce. Martin Luther King, Jr. described the beloved community in his sermons and philosophical writings as a society based on justice, equal opportunity, and love of one's fellow human beings.

from John Polkinghorne, a physicist and an Anglican priest, bolstered my resolve to enjoy this project fully.

> I cannot claim to be more than a scientist with serious theological interests. I have to say that I wish I met a few more theologians who have serious scientific interests. The interdisciplinary field of encounter between the scientific and theological world-views... calls from all its participants for a certain acceptance of risk and a certain charity towards the efforts of others with different backgrounds.[5]

Eventually, others will enter this disciplinary intersection. As our knowledge about the nature of the life space increases, liberation theologians will have to reconsider their paradigms of justice. Linear goals and hierarchical social constructs do not fit within the context of a dynamic and indeterminate world. Some initial wariness of scientific languages is expected, given the history of pseudoscientific doctrines that supported and purportedly verified racism's mythologies. However, today's findings in physics and cosmology offer the opportunity to transform narratives of violation into a more tenable perspective on human identity and relationality.

The most apparent risk on this interdisciplinary journey is that of obsolescence. Theories in physics and cosmology are emerging and receding with alarming regularity. However, this dynamism encourages those who work at the intersection of culture, religion, and science to avoid arrogant assumptions about permanence, for we only know in part. This is what I hope to accomplish: I hope that ordinary people like me will hear the powerful metaphors, symbols, and "words of power"[6] that emerge from physics and cosmology as a clarion call to broaden our thinking about origins, endings, and the process of moral fulfillment.

Quantum worlds and cosmological findings offer compelling

---

5. John Polkinghorne, "From Physicist to Priest," in *Science and Theology: The New Consonance*, ed. Ted Peters (Boulder, CO: Westview, 1998), 59.

6. This phrase is taken from Edward Farley's discussion in *Deep Symbols: Their Postmodern Effacement and Reclamation* (Harrisburg, PA: Trinity Press International, 1996), 1.

perspectives of the human journey. Moreover, experts in the sciences and theology are making profound connections between technological formulations and everyday life. I am astounded by the synthesis that cosmologist Brian Swimme and scientific writer Angela Tilby have accomplished, the verve and brilliance of astrophysicist Vera Rubin and astronaut Mae Jemison, the ability of physicists Michio Kaku, Neil deGrasse Tyson, and Brian Greene to speak to common folks, and the challenges offered by cosmologists Stephen Hawking, David Bohm, and Carl Sagan.

African American women also contributed to explorations of the cosmos. Mathematician Katherine Johnson calculated orbital mechanics critical to the success of space flights. Beth A. Brown (1969–2008) was an astronomer who worked at NASA on the multiwavelength research of elliptical galaxies. There are people of every ilk and origin who have looked toward the stars with wonder, curiosity, and determination.

To be certain, we are all treading new ground. These astronomers/physicists are also culturists; some are inclined toward religion and most believe that the ramparts that have been erected between the disciplines ought to be dismantled. Why quibble about who should have the authority to talk about what, when we are receiving information about our universe that is so startling, we hardly know where to file it? As the mysteries abound, I turn to the work of theologian Edward Farley (1929–2014), who said this about the task before us: "We are not given so much a cognitive victory over the mysteries of life as occasional illuminations against a huge backdrop of puzzlement."[7] Puzzlement may be the beacon that sustains our search for the good life.

From the intersection of theology, cosmology, physics, and culture emerges a view of human life that is not divided neatly along categories of race, ethnicity, class, and sexual orientation. Instead, human life on quantum and cosmic levels evinces a oneness that is not dependent on religious hope or social plan. It is an intrinsic element of a universe that is both staggering and healing in its human/divine scope.

7. Ibid., 63.

one

⁘

Awakening into the fullness
of the present yields unrestrained intimacy;
awakening into the present is communion;
but one awakens from despair, not from self-gratification.
Despair shouldn't be cultivated, just allowed to surface.
Being useless uncovers despair, and the same empowerment
occurs when the optimist ceases to grasp at the future,
when the mourner ceases to grasp at the past,
or when the bereft ceases to grasp at
what might have been.

—Jim Corbett,
Goatwalking: A Guide to Wildland Living

⁘

Coming to Awareness:
Staying Woke!

Knowing has consequences.
—Emilie M. Townes, *Womanist Ethics and the Cultural Production of Evil*

We cannot un-know what we know. Our eyes have been opened.
We cannot un-see what we have seen.
—Peter Birkenhead, "With Eyes Wide Open"

I AM DEVOTING THIS early chapter to a discussion of awareness because it seems that our connections to the cosmos and our commitments to one another are fading from the horizon of collective purpose. By this I mean that, except during times of national tragedy and crisis, we are not paying attention to the decline of our social covenants. While there are exceptions to this sweeping statement, few would disagree that radical individualism has proven to be an intoxicating lure in Western cultures. Some consider it to be the rambunctious offspring of capitalism, but it is also a lifestyle choice for those who have been disappointed by collective dreams.

The dreams of which I speak were conjured by the prophets of the Civil Rights movement. Dream language served a worthy purpose for people who were denied land, language, culture, identity, and autonomy. Moreover, it helped formerly enslaved people to grasp the elusive contours of liberation by first envisioning themselves as empowered and whole. However, decades later, most of the dreams are still dreams and nothing more.

It is time to awaken to self, society, and the cosmos, for none of us has the luxury of sleepwalking through impending cultural and scientific revolutions. In the last sermon that he preached before he was assassinated, Martin Luther King, Jr. urged us to "remain awake through a great revolution."[1]

This chapter explores awareness as a personal, rhetorical, theological, and scientific process. It is the attempt to stir the imagination, awaken the slumbering idea of mutuality, and connect our "dreams" of a reconciled society with scientific observations about the nature of the universe.

Awakening to the Present

WE FUNCTION IN A WORLD that seems familiar until sleep, disaster, death, or wonder causes us to shift our gaze. On those occasions, we glimpse a spectrum of realities that defy the limits of our language. These infrequent but spellbinding events confront us with mystery, a profound helplessness, and a repulsion/attraction to know more. Yet, for purposes of sanity, the human community implicitly agrees that certain conceptual boundaries will be drawn. We will explore and create, destroy and describe, but we will not include certain facts or discourses in our everyday lives.

The more important excluded facts are that we can't escape death and we are living and interacting with others on a planet that is hurtling

---

1. This phrase is taken from the sermon given on Passion Sunday, March 31, 1968, at the National Cathedral in Washington, DC, and reprinted in James M. Washington, ed., *A Testament of Hope: The Essential Writings and Speeches of Martin Luther King, Jr.* (San Francisco: HarperCollins, 1986), 268–278. See also Barbara A. Holmes and the Honorable Susan Holmes Winfield, "King, the Constitution, and the Courts: Remaining Awake Through a Great Revolution," in *The Legacy of Martin Luther King, Jr.: The Boundaries of Law, Politics, and Religion*, ed. Lewis V. Baldwin (Notre Dame, IN: University of Notre Dame Press, 2002).

RACE AND THE COSMOS

through space, dodging asteroids and other cosmic disasters. If allowed to inhabit daily conversations, such realities wreak havoc with the simple pleasures of life. To fend off such startling realizations, we weave gossamer webs of habit and familiarity that lull, sustain, and entangle us.

But it is difficult to articulate creative solutions to intransigent problems while dazed. As a result, many have given up on the hope of a flourishing multicultural society. We can't seem to hold on to the vision, and, on those rare occasions when we can, there seem to be so few liberating words to describe the future.

Yet, while we despair within the rhetorical boxes that we have created, there are scientific discourses that have not been incorporated into our visions of liberation. To situate the struggle for justice within cosmological contexts may invigorate stalled discussions about the "good life."

Awakening to the Cosmos

Up ABOVE OUR HEADS, there are worlds unknown and a canopy of grace, light, air, and water that supports our survival. Without realizing it, we expend massive amounts of energy to block out the vastness of our universe. This is to be expected, for, in its totality, this information can be more than human systems can take. However, by riveting our attention on the mundane, we filter out the wonder that is available with each breath.

Although we have a fascination with space and the possibility of life in other realms, we steadfastly refuse to respond when the universe invites us to broaden our lines of sight. We are beckoned by blazing sunsets and the pictures returned by powerful telescopic lenses, yet, on any given day, we court a busyness that beguiles us into focusing on the limited perspectives in our immediate space.

Today, scientific information about the universe is increasing exponentially while ethnic and racial balances within the United States are shifting radically. In the scientific realm, the epistemological foundations for hierarchy, dominance, and rationality are crumbling, while proponents of gender, class, and sexual equity have found their public voices.

Attention Must Be Paid

COMING TO AWARENESS implies some level of sustained attentiveness. We are not paying attention to the activities of hate groups, racists, and terrorists until disaster strikes. We can't hear the cry for attention from our children until a gun is fired in a classroom. In the aftermath of the inevitable, members of the media document our confusion as to the causes of our inattention. In the words of Linda Loman in the play *Death of a Salesman*, "Attention must be paid."[2]

What would it mean to put the thirty-year mortgage; the war in one European, Balkan, Asian, African, or Middle Eastern nation; or the dips and crests of the stock market in a cosmic context? To consider our lives within the scope of a planetary system that is billions of years old would put our race/class/gender scuffles into perspective. To realize the rarity of blue/green life-sustaining planets in the cosmos would put ecology on the top of the priority list.

The miracle of the human self is that we can hold many visions and ideas simultaneously. However, we cannot act on every front. Priorities order our actions. When we can't act directly, we delegate authority to institutions so that they can act on our behalf. However, in much the same way that we approach nature as inert scenery, we have also assumed that institutions are empty repositories of our will. New Testament scholar Walter Wink (1935–2012) penned an extraordinary series on the "powers" that helps to change that perception.[3] Wink made the case that institutions have a socio-spiritual nature. Once set in motion, "they can only be fundamentally changed by addressing that interiority."[4]

Jesus is depicted as one who is aware of the inner life of institutions. When he wants changes in the church, he does not call a meeting or talk to clergy. Instead, in the Book of Revelation (see 2:1–3, for example), he

---

2. Arthur Miller, *Death of a Salesman* (New York: ICM Partners, 1949, 1980), 40.

3. See Walter Wink, *Engaging the Powers: Discernment and Resistance in a World of Domination* (Minneapolis: Fortress, 1992); *Naming the Powers: The Language of Power in the New Testament* (Minneapolis: Fortress, 1984); *The Powers That Be: Theology for a New Millennium* (Minneapolis: Fortress, 1998); *Unmasking the Powers: The Invisible Forces That Determine Human Existence* (Minneapolis: Fortress, 1986); and *When the Powers Fall: Reconciliation in the Healing of Nations* (Minneapolis: Fortress, 1998).

4. Wink, *Engaging the Powers*, 84.

addresses the "angel" or the socio-spiritual nature of the institution. Systems analysts agree with Wink that institutions can act with an autonomy that manifests itself as socio-spiritual intent. In fact, the interiority of social institutions may offer an explanation for the social outcomes that no one seems to will or want.

Does anyone really want police officers to act as an occupying force in blighted and impoverished neighborhoods? Do we really want weapons orbiting over our head in space? I don't think that we want our legal system to offer one standard of justice to the rich and another to the poor, or our health and economic systems to neglect children and the elderly. But they do, and are continuing to do so, in our names and on our behalf, yet we are dumbfounded as to the forces we have unleashed.

In this respect and in others, the lack of personal and public awareness is profound. Our vision is narrowed by the pursuit of happiness and economic stability. In myopic bliss, we toil with our eyes cast downward, oblivious to the wonders above and within, and numbed to the need for activism.

When we are fully alert in spirit, mind, and body, we are more than we imagine and can accomplish more than we suppose. Moments of awareness occur as a dawning of meaning, when the familiar suddenly becomes infused with new insights or unfamiliar ideas merge with the wellspring of experiences and beliefs that pervade human consciousness. Such occasions feel like personal discoveries. While in the midst of an epiphany, folks inevitably apply the term "discovery" to lands, people, and ideas that have always been present. We use the language of strange and alien sightings when the more accurate statement would be, "Eureka! I have just awakened to a long-standing reality that an inner unveiling has finally allowed me to see." Unexpectedly, these moments of awareness can break into fixed belief systems and perspectival narratives that are incorporated into the very essence of our being from birth.

An awakening is necessary to reconnect us to our origins and one another. Epiphanous understandings may develop as we contemplate personal and collective orientations toward the cosmos.

Awareness Is Personal

IN THE AFRICAN AMERICAN community, a history of resistance to domination seems to make the call to an awakening unnecessary. Yet communal responsiveness to the collective context of oppression neglected the devastating long-term personal effects. Despite resistance, overcoming, the development of internal bonds of trust, and ostensible social, political, and economic advances, many African Americans still struggle with issues of identity. I want to focus on two aspects of the struggle: double/multiple consciousness and nihilism.

Double/multiple consciousness

> The Negro is a sort of seventh son[/daughter], born with a veil, and gifted with second-sight in this American world—a world which yields him[/her] no true self-consciousness but only lets him[/her] see himself[/herself] through the revelation of the other world.
> —W. E. B. Du Bois, *The Souls of Black Folk*

W. E. B. Du Bois (1868–1963) described "double consciousness" as a limitation and a lack of self-awareness. If one can only access "self" through the eyes of an Afrocentric-despising culture, what hope is left? Theologian Henry Young offers a similar interpretation of the phrase. He says,

> Double-consciousness means always to look at oneself through the eyes of others, to measure oneself by the cultural standards of the majority social group, which in this country looks at Afro-Americans with "amused contempt and pity," refusing to yield to Afro-Americans their own, true self-consciousness.[5]

Young also identifies the African American struggle as the effort to become authentic selves.[6] The problem with attaining this goal seems to

---

5. Henry James Young, *Hope in Process: A Theology of Social Pluralism* (Minneapolis: Fortress, 1990), 2–3. Young's argument is based on W. E. B. Du Bois' discussion in *The Souls of Black Folk* (New York: Fawcett, 1968), 17.

6. Young, *Hope in Process*, 3.

be a continuing focus on fulfillment within the social limitations imposed by dominant culture. According to Young, a perpetual modality of "overcoming" seems to foreclose the possibility of true self-consciousness.

And yet, one need not enter the fray on this phantom battlefield. The antidote to the generational trauma of POC is found in the rejection of dualistic thinking and the acceptance of a multiplicity of identities and social locations. To wed self-acceptance to national standards rather than spiritual and cosmological realities is an exercise in futility.

Although Du Bois described imposed impediments to self-awareness within the context of American society, I want to offer another viewpoint. Double or multiple consciousness can be a special gift of insight, wisdom, and perspective. In my family's Gullah traditions, being "born with the veil" is a sign of second sight, a super power that allows the recipient to see beyond this world into others. It is a gift of cosmic importance.

The veil is not an obstruction. Instead, it heightens a person's ability to see what cannot be seen by the naked eye. To be aware of one's circumstances and to be able to access multiple dimensions is very freeing. If, in fact, a person situated in the liminal regions of culture and society as a result of ethnic origin, skin color, gender/sexual identification, or any other marginalizing trait also has the same cosmic gifts as a person born with the veil, then they are gifted beyond measure.[7] Therein lies the hope of POC. Freedom is reclaimed through the spiritual and ancestral gifts of second sight, and communal narratives of empowerment that create connections to every living thing.

Nihilism

It was Cornel West's discussion of race[8] that awakened us to the personal consequences of oppression. Race matters not just because an

---

7. Law professor Patricia Williams refers to the phenomenon as "multiple voice, double-voicedness—the shifting consciousness which is the daily experience of people of color and women," from "Response to Mari Matsuda: 1988 Women of Color and the Law Conference at Yale University," *Women's Rights Law Reporter* 14 (1992), 299. See also Shannon Gilreath, "Toward a Multiple Consciousness of Language: A Tribute to Professor Mari Matsuda," *Michigan Law Review* 112 (2014), https://repository.law.umich.edu/mlr_fi/vol112/iss1/11/.

8. Cornel West, *Race Matters* (New York: Vintage, 1994).

esteemed professor can't get a taxicab, but because it assigns inferiority in ways that can't be ignored or overcome. Those who suffer from the residual effects of discrimination and oppression tend to be disintegrating selves. Cornel West's definition of nihilism is pertinent to this discussion and to the issue of race and identity in North America.

He says that nihilism in this context exceeds philosophical understandings. "Nihilism is to be understood here not as a philosophic doctrine that there are not rational grounds for legitimate standards or authority; it is, far more, the lived experience of coping with a life of horrifying meaninglessness, hopelessness, and (most important) lovelessness."[9] Over long periods of time, the results are catastrophic. Symptoms include, but are not limited to, violence and detachment from the human community.[10]

Nihilism can also spawn a paradoxical identity stance. For example, when the movements for justice began, the terms "superiority" and "inferiority" predominated. Today, few would describe themselves as "inferior." In fact, the word "inferiority" seems archaic. To listen to the rhetoric of the ghetto, the streets, the underclass, there is not a single person or ethnic group left in the West who claims inferiority as an accurate description of themselves. This would be a good thing if there were not so many examples of self-denigration and self-destructive behavior among those same individuals and groups. Perhaps our personal awareness is skewed. According to psychologist Carl G. Jung (1875–1961),

> If an inferiority is conscious, one always has a chance to correct it. Furthermore, it is constantly in contact with other interests, so that it is steadily subjected to modifications. But if it is repressed and isolated from consciousness, it never gets corrected. It is, moreover, liable to burst forth in a moment of unawareness. At all events, it forms an unconscious snag, blocking the most well-meant attempts.[11]

---

9. Ibid., 22.
10. Ibid.
11. Carl G. Jung, *Psychology and Religion* (New Haven: Yale University Press, 1938, 1966), 93.

RACE AND THE COSMOS

Awareness of our snags, blockages, and inferiorities cannot be suppressed without risking catastrophic personal and social consequences. To admit that we are hurting, despite the passage of time, would begin the process of healing. Our collective wounds around issues of race and identity are deep and festering. Nihilism is rampant. We are in need of renewal and a turn to joint purposes. West suggests that "nihilism is a disease of the soul. It can never be completely cured, and there is always the possibility of relapse. But there is always a chance for conversion—a chance for people to believe that there is hope for the future and a meaning to struggle."[12]

The pronouncement is both dire and hopeful. Conversion implies the necessity of self-definition and is synonymous with a turning from false and negative images of selfhood toward images of wholeness that reflect the divinity in all of us. Conversion also implies abandoning the hope that POC will be loved by those who never loved us. It requires release of the yearning for reconciliation in favor of the healing of community trauma.[13]

This is not a resurgence of Afro-pessimism. It is a practical response to an intransigent issue. We only have so much energy and time on this earth. It should not be spent knocking on doors that, if opened, will simply slam shut as the cyclical nature of oppression requires or as cultural and political winds blow. Perhaps conversion can be facilitated by the use of analogies borrowed from physics and cosmology that emphasize sources of energy, potential, and belonging.

Personhood and science

The previous discussion focused on identity issues within specific social contexts; however, we cannot understand personhood fully without the addition of theological and scientific discourses. We need these disciplinary prisms to capture the many facets of identity because

---

12. West, *Race Matters*, 29.

13. In the 25th anniversary edition of his book, West offers a new introduction. In it, he claims that events in Baltimore, Ferguson, and Charlottesville are evidence of imperial and moral decline that invites civic resistance; i.e. the Black Lives Matter Movement and Standing Rock.

personhood is not a static category. Instead, it is a dynamic response to culture, experience, and encoded physical predispositions. These tendencies seem to be congruent with events in the quantum world.

The quantum world is one of potential rather than actuality. Unexpected effects are the norm rather than the exception and the observer can affect outcomes significantly. In a similar fashion, fluctuations of unity and disunity are characteristic of personhood. When I describe the process in this way, it seems like a return to dualisms that reached a peak in the theories of a mind/body split. However, like quantum events, unity and disunity are not polar opposites, but fields of possibility and potential that become available in ways that are not specifically predictable.

The idea of disunity speaks to the multiple aspects of personality and self that emerge and recede. Unity speaks to the ways in which disparate thoughts, perceptions, memories, and actions are integrated into a retrievable reservoir of cohesive information and inspiration that can't be located in any physical process. Danah Zohar offers this response to the puzzle of consciousness:

> "I" am not my rebellious side or my conventional side; both are aspects of me. Nor am "I" the various brain events that give rise to jiggling in the molecules of my neuron cell walls. Quantum systems *can't* be reduced in that way. The unity of the quantum self is a *substantial* unity, a thing in itself that exists in its own right. And the strength of the self at any moment, the amount of awareness and attention that "I" can bring to bear on my environment or my relationship with others, depends entirely on the extent to which my subselves (my many pockets of awareness) are integrated at that moment.[14]

The most basic act of awareness is to recognize self as a unity. The inability to do so indicates a profound cognitive disorder. But this unity is not reduced to immutable traits or characteristics that define who is

14. Danah Zohar, *The Quantum Self: Human Nature and Consciousness Defined by the New Physics* (New York: William Morrow, 1990), 115. See also an African perspective in Rasheeda Phillips, ed., *Black Quantum Futurism: Theory and Practice*, Vol. 1 (Philadelphia: AfroFuturist Affair, 2015).

or is not human. It is a unity in plurality that allows for the emergence of self on many levels. Roles assigned by civic mythologies can fracture this unity. This is particularly true when issues of race, gender, class, or sexuality circumscribe our roles.

We may not be able to solve problems of race, identity, and the moral life with legal and social integration, but we must be integrated selves to grasp the multiple aspects of the problem. As evolving selves, we are identified by the vicissitudes of current and past realities and relationships. We are also linked and defined by an expanding and diversified cosmos. In the midst of these connections, human awareness is a gift of personal and communal potential.

That awareness is the promise that we are open systems, created with the ability to recognize our limitations and the potential for transcendence.[15] This openness and sentience is not unique; it may be a manifestation of normative aspects of the cosmos. In this respect, science writer Angela Tilby says, "our presence in the universe is very closely linked to the way the universe is. There is a resonance between the existence of human beings and the world within which we are embedded and from which we have emerged."[16] She envisions the human journey as one that is permeated by ongoing moments of self-assessment. Physicist Paul Davies agrees and says that "the order in nature is characterized by *contingent intelligibility*"; he refers to "an intellectual as well as a physical component to nature."[17] Moreover, he implies that human intelligence is a subset of a divine intelligence that is manifested in the physical world.

According to Davies, "The brain is the medium of expression of the human mind. Similarly, the entire universe would be the medium of expression of the mind of a natural God."[18] Theologian Karl Rahner (1904–1984) suggested that "human beings represent the cosmos come to consciousness of itself."[19] He also proposed that God may have created

---

15. Angela Tilby, *Soul: God, Self and the New Cosmology* (New York: Doubleday, 1993), 191–193.

16. Ibid., 216.

17. Paul Davies, "Is the Universe Absurd?" in *Science and Theology: The New Consonance*, ed. Ted Peters (Boulder, CO: Westview, 1998), 67.

18. Paul Davies, *God and the New Physics* (New York: Simon and Schuster, 1983), 223.

19. Karl Rahner, *Foundations of Christian Faith* (New York: Seabury, 1978), 188–189.

matter that always has the potential to be self-transcendent or self-aware and in relationship with others.

If this is true, then we are participants in a story that is cosmic in scope but very personal. For the two-thirds world, this means that personal stories of oppression are not unique historical markers that constrain and limit. Rather, the stories delineate the events and itinerary of emergent beings in an enfolding/unfolding life space.

Awareness Is Rhetorical

RHETORIC IS A VEHICLE for transformation. Oppressed people in any society dream and whisper about liberation long before deliverance comes. During the 1960s, talk of reconciliation dominated most social conversations. These conversations ended when racial violence continued despite (or maybe as the result of) the election of the first African American president. Our inability to solve the problems of racial discord may be due in part to the ways in which we have discussed the issue. Unwittingly, we have talked racial reconciliation into the realm of "someday," where it remains in suspended animation.

The importance of public discourse about difficult social issues cannot be overemphasized. Public dialogue infuses an issue with energy. According to Yi-Fu Tuan, "Humans use language not so much to convey factual information as to construct worlds, illuminating certain facets of reality while throwing others into the shade."[20] If Yi-Fu Tuan is correct, our languages construct worlds that harm and help in particular ways.

Those who are deemed worthy of support receive it; those who are deemed pariahs do not. Moreover, preliminary determinations as to which ethnic groups are valued can be ascertained by listening to the pool of analogies, metaphors, and anecdotes that describe them.

Given this reality, cultural theorist Marimba Ani urges the members of the Africana community to find new ways to describe their lives: "Ultimately, the liberation of our thought from its colonized condition will

---

20. Yi-Fu Tuan, *Passing Strange and Wonderful: Aesthetics, Nature, and Culture* (New York: Kodansha International, 1995), 7.

require the creation of a new language."[21] This suggestion gives some people pause because there have been so many descriptive name changes over the years as African Americans have struggled to define themselves.

These identifying labels have included African, colored, Negro, black, Afro-American, African American, and Africana. Although the various "becoming" labels cycled over the decades like temporary name tags, the impermanence of an identifying group label can offer an unexpected freedom. Naming is an ethereal and transitory act. Labels that purport to define a people don't reflect the truth of who they are in relation to the cosmos or one another.

However, periodic reconfigurations of language models must occur if our discourse is to reflect accurately a universe that reveals and rescinds information about the human community at regular intervals. Periodic changes are also necessary because language, like clothing, can wear thin. A good example can be found in the discourse of feminine empowerment.

Once the "patriarchy" in feminist thought was identified, the systems that sustained the phenomenon began to affirm women publicly in rhetorically superficial ways. Hiring practices were altered slightly to allow external boundaries to loosen, while the internal restrictions for movement into positions of power remained rigid. At the same time, single examples of achievement were touted as icons of accomplishments that ought to be emulated.

Meanwhile, the languages used to identify points of oppression were beginning to lose their impact. As the patriarchal pillars of injustice were named, they slipped safely out of sight and out of public consciousness. This submergence of oppression below the horizon of awareness makes those who rail against injustice seem to be tilting at windmills.

The "Me Too" movement brought these difficult issues back to the forefront of societal awareness. In 2006, Tarana Burke founded the movement and began using the phrase "Me Too" to raise awareness of the pervasiveness of sexual abuse and assault in society. The phrase "Me Too" developed into a broader movement following the 2017 use of #MeToo as a hashtag following the Harvey Weinstein sexual abuse allegations.

---

21. Marimba Ani, *Yurugu: An African-Centered Critique of European Cultural Thought and Behavior* (Trenton, NJ: Africa World Press, 1994), 10.

Burke now says that the focus of the movement has shifted to salacious details and firings that seem to pit women against men. She reminds us that Me Too is for the entire community, notwithstanding gender identification. In this instance and others,

> The use of language is as important as the use of science. . . . People's use of words plays a central role in who benefits from our knowledge and abilities, who is put at a disadvantage, who is put to flight and who is destroyed from the face of the earth. In short, the ability to use language across this entire planet and throughout a growing part of our solar system makes us substantive co-creators of life and death.[22]

Language points beyond itself and helps us to situate self and others within a context that feels familiar, even if it isn't. Novelist Al Young refers to this alternative as "actualized speech," utterances that can transcend and create new realities.[23] Young says, "words and language as actualized speech can bring a created order and world into being . . . solidify family cohesion, effect profound curative effects, and transmute perception, consciousness, and empirical reality (as with hoodoo or conjure traditions)."[24]

Language also helps to orient us toward the spiritual realm. The Holy Scriptures are full of references to actualized speech. God speaks and the world changes, then Jesus is described as the Word, and the Holy Spirit is described as the one who utters the unutterable desires of the heart in prayer. Those who claim Christian beliefs have a history of rhetorical performance that drags reality from behind the narrative scrim into the local context. But then what?

As responsive readers of a history that permeates and influences the present, we are required to add our own discourses to the mix. The question is whether our languages are congruent with our lives. Rhetorical

22. Vernon K. Robbins, "The Present and Future of Rhetorical Analysis," in *The Rhetorical Analysis of Scripture: Essays from the 1995 London Conference,* ed. Stanley E. Porter and Thomas H. Olbricht (Sheffield, England: Sheffield Academic Press, 1997), 24.

23. Quoted in Clarice J. Martin, "Somebody Done Hoodoo'd the Hoodoo Man: Language, Power, Resistance, and the Effective History of Pauline Texts in American Slavery," *Semeia* 83/84 (1998), 205.

24. Ibid.

scholar Peter du Preez reminds us that "every way of life has a kind of talk associated with it. Nazi life, apartheid life, anarchist life, Buddhist life, even horse-racing life."[25] Perhaps the advent of the beloved community is delayed due to the lack of talk that specifically delineates its territory. Can such a spectacular vision be manifested when we don't share collective expectations for the project? Du Preez gives examples of "talk" so specific that it crystallizes human action and sanitizes heinous deeds.

> The talk associated with a way of life evolves with it, accompanies it every step of the way. It constitutes intentions. . . . The second thing that talk does is to provide reasons or permissions for the action. When we are asked why it is so difficult to get rid of this kind of talk, we show how heavily people invest in it. To change their talk is often to change their way of life.[26]

This is the problem. Despite our protestations to the contrary, we still talk in ways that support racism. We have inherited some of the discourses of difference from pseudoscientific theories. The theories of biological taxonomist Carolus Linnaeus (1707–1778) provide a good example. Linnaeus divided the human family into color categories (red, yellow, white, and black) and attributed particular character traits to each. Europeans were vested with the adult capacities of morality, perseverance, toughness, faith, and civilization, while Africans were considered childlike, happy, and carefree, with no incentive to improve their lot in life.[27]

Inevitably, comparisons were made between the alleged incapacities of women and purportedly inferior races. Women were deemed to be

25. Peter du Preez, "Reason Which Cannot Be Reasoned With: What Is Public Debate and How Does It Change?" in *Empirical Logic and Public Debate: Essays in Honour of Else M. Barth,* ed. Erick C. W. Krabbe, Renee Jose Dalitz, and Pier A. Smit (Atlanta: Rodopi, 1993), 211. See also National Public Radio, "Rhetoric, Racism and Rage: A Violent Week in America," *NPR,* October 29, 2018, https://www.npr.org/2018/10/29/661855581/rhetoric-racism-and-rage-a-violent-week-in-america.

26. Ibid.

27. Stephen Jay Gould, "American Polygeny and Craniometry before Darwin," in *The "Racial" Economy of Science: Toward a Democratic Future,* ed. Sandra Harding (Bloomington, IN: Indiana University Press, 1993), 87–88. See Paul R. Ehrlich and S. Shirley Feldman, *The Race Bomb: Skin Color, Prejudice, and Intelligence* (New York: Quadrangle, 1977), 16, for a discussion of Linnaeus' *Systema Naturae.*

like slaves and children; Africans were like apes and children. As science purported to support the idea of biological inferiority, metaphorical systems and facile analogies structured that information in ways that helped to create inferiority as an objective reality.[28] When it became politically incorrect to espouse these ideas, they were removed from public but not private discourse.

Silence cannot be expected to replace entrenched and oppressive language systems. Nor will vague musings about "overcoming one day" rectify decades of damage. To make those assumptions assures that there will be no material changes. When we change our talk, we change our way of life. Only then can we project images that more accurately reflect our assessments of self, others, and our place in the world.

Borrowing languages from the sciences to enlighten and describe the human condition is not new. Whether we realize it or not, our social institutions, laws, theological perspectives, and even personal relationships reflect our views of the universe. As physicist Nick Herbert notes, the simile "the world is a giant clock" translated the basic elements of Newtonian physics, "namely, atomicity, objectivity and determinism," into mechanistic and hierarchical social relations and institutional structures.[29]

Inevitably, the rigidity of a universe that operated like a giant clock was reflected in political and social initiatives that supported the divine right of kings and justified the oppression of indigenous cultures. Those who were attempting to align the social world with the presumed order of the universe soon controlled those who were deemed illogical, anti-intellectual, and incapable of rational perspectives. Given these historical facts, one wonders how rhetoric that emanates from a discipline dominated by those deemed to be dominators can be used to open closed perspectives about race and identity.

It is certainly true that scientific languages are no more objective than any other form of human communication. They are also laden with

28. See Nancy Leys Stepan, "Race and Gender: The Role of Analogy in Science," in *The "Racial" Economy of Science: Toward a Democratic Future,* ed. Sandra Harding (Bloomington, IN: Indiana University Press, 1993), 359–376.

29. Nick Herbert, *Quantum Reality: Beyond the New Physics* (New York: Anchor, 1985), xi.

cultural assumptions that encode biased practices. However, the new physics and cosmology offer a view of humanity, consciousness, and the life space that cannot be confined by oppression's cultural snares. Moreover, the findings point beyond our learned limitations. Our task is to wake up and "stay woke."

Summary

WE ARE NOT hamsters on a wheel, waiting to fall into the cedar shavings at the bottom of the cage. We are seekers of light and life, bearers of shadows and burdens. We are struggling to journey together toward moral fulfillment. We are learning to embrace the unfathomable darkness where God dwells with enthusiasm that equals our love of light. Physics and cosmology have metaphors and languages to help us awaken to these and other possibilities.

The suggestion that we add complex scientific theories to our daily to-do list may seem ludicrous to those who are already overwhelmed. In truth, daily life can be exhausting. We blame our jobs and relationships for the never-ending cycle of stress and discontent. Yet, we never consider that this ever-deepening reservoir of fatigue may be the direct result of our lack of attention to a bigger cosmic picture.

When we are fully aware, we realize that socially constructed models of human flourishing only provide a starting place. We are not just citizens of one nation or another, but of the human and cosmic community.

Awareness is the moment when we rise with eyes crusted from self-induced dreams of control, domination, victimization, and self-hatred to catch a glimpse of the divine in the face of "the other." Then God's self-identification, "I am that I am / I will be who I will be" (Exodus 3:14), becomes a liberating example of awareness, mutuality, and self-revelation.

Jim Corbett, goatwalker, activist, and co-founder of the sanctuary movement, said it better than I can: "Awakening into the present is communion."[30] Awakening into the present is also an awakening into the past and the future. It is the opportunity to engage the visceral and

30. Jim Corbett, *Goatwalking: A Guide to Wildland Living, a Quest for the Peaceable Kingdom* (New York: Viking, 1991), 6.

visionary aspects of life, to glimpse the mysterious in the ordinary, to be liberated from external and internal constraints. The next chapter discusses the liberation project, its rhetorical legacy, its successes and failures, and its future.

two

Because black life is fundamentally determined
by black suffering and resistance to whiteness (the power of nonbeing),
black existence is without the possibility of transcendence
from the blackness that whiteness created.
Without transcendence from the determinancy of whiteness,
black theology's promise of liberation remains existentially
a function of black self-consciousness. . . .
The promise of black liberation remains bracketed
both existentially and politically.

—Victor Anderson,
Beyond Ontological Blackness

⠿

Oppressive language does more than represent violence;
it is violence;
does more than represent the limits of knowledge;
it limits knowledge.

—Toni Morrison,
1993 Nobel Lecture

⠿

Liberation Theology and Beyond

Liberation theology is simply the latest gimmick to keep minority groups circling the wagons with the vain hope that they can eliminate the oppression that surrounds them. It does not seek to destroy the roots of oppression, but merely to change the manner in which oppression manifests itself.

—Vine Deloria, Jr., *For This Land: Writings on Religion in America*

VINE DELORIA, JR. (1933–2005) was not alone in his retrospective suspicion of the entire liberation project. The liberation movements were supposed to "set the captives free" (Luke 4:18), but can people be free if they are released from one set of limitations into another, from a box into a maze? The idea of freedom had no real content for the activists, except for the content borrowed from the political, theological, and economic suppositions of the dominant culture. To view the world differently requires a transformative view of liberation. Without this view, we are left with memorable tunes and unfinished business.

It is not so much that liberation theology failed; rather, it is that the political and theological aspects of the movement veered from expected outcomes. Marxism died an unexpected and ignominious death. Socialism, in its early twentieth-century form, lingered, then disappeared until Senator Bernie Sanders and Representative Alexandria Ocasio-Cortez resurrected its democratic format.

Charismatic Christians in South America made inroads into Catholic territory and Catholic authorities were confronted with systemic child abuse scandals. Liberals became more conservative, conservatives got talk shows and religion (but not in that order), and money became more alluring than utopian real estate in the community-called-beloved.

I am suggesting that the language we currently use to describe and envision liberation has lost its vitality. Words like "oppression" and "victimization" that once incited and inspired us now only have the ability to make us weary. Like a knife that loses its sharpness in the effort to cut through rigidity, the discourse of liberation was dulled in the effort to dispel deeply sedimented concepts of inferiority and superiority in North American culture. Today, more is needed. If a just and reconciled community is to become a reality in the coming years, new ideas and languages will be needed to break the cycles of oppression and domination that persist in North America.

As political scientist Daniel H. Levine points out, "It is a mistake to confuse liberation theology with liberation itself."[1] The question for the next generation is whether we should move beyond the discourse of liberation or refine rhetoric, goals, and methods of the movement to reflect current issues. Even as I write this proposal, I am wondering what it means to speak of moving beyond the discourses of liberation theology.

Is there anything beyond the languages of journey, resistance, and overcoming? In one respect, we can't move beyond that which was never finished, if a finish is ever possible for those who seek freedom. From 2017 through 2019, liberation movements are being revitalized through the #MeToo initiative, Black Lives Matter, and the LGBTQIA+'s quests for equal rights. Each movement includes elements of previous activism but presents different leadership and strategies.

From my point of view, one problematic aspect of the Civil Rights movement was its commitment to unending struggle and ongoing battle

1. Daniel H. Levine, "The Future of Liberation Theology," *Journal of the International Institute* 2, no. 2 (Winter 1995): 1–3. See also James H. Cone, *A Black Theology of Liberation* (Maryknoll, NY: Orbis, 2010).

readiness. This is a noble commitment to free a people from hangings, apartheid, and genocide, but one that engenders a particular stance toward the world. When struggle becomes the main construct of human life, reality tends to be saturated with tension, a guarded awareness, limited communications, overachieving, and an inability to connect to other realities.

Those who are locked into this cycle continue to answer the call to arms long after the battles are over and often before they're begun. A one-sided focus on protest without its corollary of restoration locks ethnic communities into cycles of protest, but life should not be one battle after another. To move on, we must understand what we've come through.

A Black Theology of Liberation

WHEN I WAS a young teen, the first stage of the black theology project was a period of activism and spiritual resolve. I remember riding with my father, Thomas Samuel Holmes, on a bus from New Haven, Connecticut, to Selma, Alabama.

We were answering the call of Martin Luther King, Jr. to put our bodies on the line. In the previous weeks, King and his supporters had been unable to finish the march in Alabama, as they were beaten and attacked by local and state law enforcement. On this second march, the streets swelled with people of every ethnic origin, determined to reach the state capital and demand freedom.

Local people in the black community provided shelter in homes and small churches, and there seemed to be a festival atmosphere. The evening began with music and a gathering of activist singers and movie stars. Federalized troops, tanks, and helicopters made us feel as if we were safe, and calypso singer and activist Harry Belafonte seemed to be in charge of everything. I wondered about the twists of fate that would allow folk singer Joan Baez and I to sleep in the same southern town. She probably slept in a hotel; we curled up on cots in the basement of an old church, drank lemonade, and ate thick slabs of pound cake.

All was well, until late at night when the Klan rode. Kicking up dust, they tore through the church parking lot shouting obscenities and shooting guns into the air. At that time, the troops seemed far too far away. In response, the men from the church, ours and theirs, sat outside in their undershirts and formed a shield of sheer resolve. The women reassured us and sat just inside of the church doors as a second line of defense, with their church fans and potato-salad spoons gripped in purposeful hands. When the sun finally came up, we were glad. In the morning, we marched.

Oh, how we marveled at the hatred, the spittle, the exposed genitals and urine aimed in our direction. To be hated so completely was almost a relief. There it was for the world to see! We had not been paranoid and deluded; this was what the struggle had opposed from the beginning. On the way out of town, as march participant Viola Liuzzo (1925–1965) was being killed, we pressed down against the floor of the bus, listening to gun shots and shouts as angry locals sped past with horns blaring.

On the heels of this public activism, James Cone (1938–2018) and others translated the years of embodied protest and suffering into black theological discourse. His rhetoric was a theological response to the black power movement and an exposé of the inherent hypocrisy of a "white" theology that excluded all other perspectives. The question for African Americans was whether Christianity could emerge from its racist trappings and evince a relevance that could sustain and empower black people. Idolatrous white Christianity, introduced during slavery, could not fill that bill. As James Cone aptly noted, "In America . . . the Christian tradition is identified with the structures of racism in their oppression of black people."[2]

Since it seemed that racism and segregation were fungal appendages to the gospel, Cone reexamined Holy Scripture to find the essence of Christianity. As spokesperson for the new order, he proclaimed that Christianity is synonymous with liberation. But it was more than liberation; a gauntlet had been thrown down. Cone proclaimed that African Americans were made in the image of a black Jesus. Whether it was ontology or metaphor, Cone's declaration changed the discourse of theology forever.

Other voices were heard. William R. Jones (1933–2012) is one, who asked the unthinkable question in his book *Is God a White Racist? A Preamble to Black Theology.* The premise is unsettling. When you grow

2. James Cone, *Risks of Faith: The Emergence of a Black Theology of Liberation, 1968–1998* (Boston: Beacon, 1999), 31.

up in pietistic African American homes with Jesus and Martin Luther King, Jr. in black velvet on the wall, you don't ask such things—but Jones did. He simply wanted to know why the emphasis is on liberation and suffering when it should be on theodicy. Jones tested the liberation theology assertion that God is on the side of the oppressed by reminding us of catastrophic historical events that suggest the possibility that some folks may not be included in God's divine favor.

Although liberation theologians had few answers for Jones, physicist and theologian John Polkinghorne seems to share Jones' concerns about theodicy. Polkinghorne wonders how "a God both all-loving and almighty could produce a creation experienced as such a vale of tears."[3] Theology instructs those of us who also wonder, to rely on God's characteristic goodness and the tenets of faith.

Jones suggests a completely different option. In the place of comforting presumptions of benevolence, he offers a "humanocentric theism," which situates responsibility and power that was once ceded to God back into the hands of the people. Jones doesn't solve the problem of liberation, injustice, or theodicy, but poses intriguing questions about the nature of God and the duty of African Americans to take responsibility for their own destiny. But can Jones' provocative question "Is God a white racist?" hold up when the languages of science are used to respond to his challenge? I refer to the presence of dark matter, dark energy, and dark flow in the universe. One wonders how the God who creates such mysterious elements—dark, pervasive, and infused with power—can be an exclusionary symbol of white racism.

Liberation discourse did not address such issues; it focused on the legal victories that seemed to encode the aims of the movement. However, this was a very unsatisfactory culmination to a movement fueled by narrative, song, and activism. The fact that the courts finally rejected some racist legal precedents did not solve the dilemma before the African American community.

James Cone wrote, "The Black Church was thus faced with a theological dilemma: Either reject Black Power as a contradiction of Christian love (and thereby join the white church in its condemnation of Black Power

---

3. John Polkinghorne, *Science and Theology: An Introduction* (Minneapolis: Fortress, 1998), 95.

advocates as un-American and unchristian), or accept Black Power as a sociopolitical expression of the truth of the gospel."[4]

The black community refused to be backed into that corner, because they knew that Martin Luther King, Jr. and Malcolm X (1925–1965) were not enemies, but opposite and similar poles of the quest for justice. Instead, they accepted both men and sang the songs of black power and of nonviolent resistance. As they sang, they looked toward a horizon where storm clouds gathered.

The Problems with Liberation Discourse

IT TOOK US awhile to realize that the discourse of liberation theology during the 1960s was exclusionary. In fact, in many ways, it sustained sexism, classism, and phobias about difference within the culture.

Where are the women?

The first hint that the religious rhetoric of liberation theology needed an overhaul came when it became apparent that liberation was being voiced as a male construct. Even the prophetic leaders Martin Luther King, Jr. and Malcolm X could not evade their own gender bias. According to Michael Eric Dyson,

> King's beliefs about women faithfully reflected the insensitivity and indifference of many black men to the plight of black women. Many black men before the seventies simply lumped together the concerns of black communities without carefully distinguishing the effects of class and gender on one's racial status.[5]

Black and Hispanic women were being invited to participate in the transformative events of liberation movements in the two Americas; however, formal leadership was reserved for the men. As unspoken

----

4. Cone, *Risks of Faith*, 40.

5. Michael Eric Dyson, *I May Not Get There with You: The True Martin Luther King, Jr.* (New York: Free Press, 2000), 199.

justification, God was described and depicted as a male icon, interested in the liberation of male leaders, and, yes, like the story of the fishes and the loaves, the women and children would also be fed.

And yet, the women also led. Rosa Parks (1913–2005) risked everything and put her nonviolent training, learned at the Highlander School, into practice by challenging the segregated transportation system in Birmingham. Fannie Lou Hamer (1917–1977) became a political activist embodying the suffering and disenfranchisement of African Americans. Ella Baker (1903–1986) and many more struggled for freedom. She proposed an organic leadership model for activism that did not rely upon the sole male charismatic leader.

The struggle for freedom is the work of the entire community. It is not commitment that is restricted by gender, sexuality, or any other category. All who hear the message are invited to respond. The spirits of Harriet Tubman, Sojourner Truth, Fannie Lou Hamer, and others restlessly urge another generation to "put their hands to the plow and don't turn back" (Luke 9:62).

Womanists, *mujeristas*, Asian, and LGBTQIA+ theologians heard and responded. They explained the tri-modal characteristics of oppression as it affected race, class, and gender, and "broke ranks" with the patriarchy. Despite a commitment to the long-term goals of freedom and justice, the women declared the discourses and methods of the male liberationist agenda to be antithetical to their purposes.

As theologian and anthropologist Linda Thomas notes, "Womanist theology associates with and disassociates itself from black (male) theology and (white) feminist theology."[6] Thomas goes on to say that white feminist theology addresses oppression from the perspective of white women in ways that do not explicate the economic and racial aspects of patriarchy. Womanist ethicist Marcia Y. Riggs agrees, and suggests in her analysis of socio-religious praxis as the crux of a liberative moral vision that womanist theologians devise an alternative vision of reality, one that differs significantly from the vision that is premised upon ideologies of domination.[7]

---

6. Linda E. Thomas, "Womanist Theology, Epistemology, and a New Anthropological Paradigm," *Cross Currents* 48, no. 4 (Summer 1998), 4.

7. Marcia Y. Riggs, *Awake, Arise, and Act: A Womanist Call for Black Liberation* (Cleveland: Pilgrim, 1994), 97.

Mujerista scholar Ada María Isasi-Díaz (1943–2012) called this choice "living into our preferred future." Male-led liberation initiatives stressed public change while urging the women to remain in the background. For the sake of the cause, they were supposed to keep their concerns private. Instead, women activists rejected the "split between the personal and the political."[8] They led and gave notice that misogynist delusions would no longer terrorize or limit feminine potential.

In recent years, a resurgence of black women's activism and leadership emerged after the death of Trayvon Martin (1995–2012), as three self-identified queer black women (Alicia Garza, Patrisse Cullors, and Opal Tometi) founded and led the Black Lives Matter movement. This time there were no soaring anthems that focused on a collective hope of "inclusion" in American society. Another generation was in charge and their simple and effective plea was "stop killing us."

The discourse of difference

Another problematic aspect of liberation discourse was that, when it emerged during the 1960s, it did not displace the rhetoric of marginalization. In fact, parallel constructs of sexist, xenophobic, and homophobic languages and practices remained in place. Shared discourses changed to reflect an awareness that antihuman language was no longer tolerated in the public sphere; however, the private rhetoric remained the same and often erupted into view in ways that startled those who accepted the shallow discourses of integration as signs of profound cultural changes.

Some of us remember the Texaco case. Anecdotal and experiential stories about discrimination in the workplace were verified when secret tapes of a top-level meeting revealed disparaging and derogatory remarks about African American employees. The remarks struck at the heart of racial discord as they included myths and negative stereotypes that were presumed to have been "overcome."

The Texaco leak occurred in the 1990s, long after the black liberation movement had consolidated gains and dispersed. Those who presumed that justice was within reach were surprised by the resilience of the

---

8. Ada María Isasi-Díaz, *Mujerista Theology* (Maryknoll, NY: Orbis, 1996), 153–157.

domination systems. Similar cases are still occurring. Recently, two black men were arrested in Starbucks for asking to use the restroom while waiting for a friend.

The last few years have seen an increasing number of white citizens calling the police for no reason when black and brown citizens are in public spaces, and communities of color are experiencing the Klan-like propensity of officers of the law to shoot unarmed people of color first and ask questions later. Our systems of justice(?) have repeatedly affirmed their right to destroy black and brown bodies with impunity.

When there are no safe spaces, when your differences are described as markers of inferiority, one defensive tactic is to focus on the differences that had been vilified and tout those differences as markers of special and heroic attributes. Victor Anderson's critique of these idolatrous forms of individual and communal empowerment is crucial to this discussion.

> When black identities are justified primarily in terms of ontological blackness, too many of the differences that genuinely signify black life and culture recede into the background. Too often the heroically representational qualities of racial genius, the cult of black masculinity, and its often brutal forms of conformity gain ascendancy.[9]

Anderson urges a broader goal of cultural fulfillment through participation in public theology and a rejection of idolatrous configurations of liberation. He contends that it is essentialist discourse and the reification of ethnic suffering and heroism that distorts the goals of liberation theology and exacerbates trauma.

The wolf and the lamb

It also became apparent that liberation models of justice assumed moral underpinnings that just didn't exist in an unjust society. If one imagines that the society in question is "the wolf," and Mexican farm workers, ethnic minorities, and descendants of slaves are the sheep, the

---

9. Victor Anderson, *Beyond Ontological Blackness: An Essay on African American Religious and Cultural Criticism* (New York: Continuum, 1999), 162.

question becomes whether the wolf who has imprisoned, enslaved, and consumed its captives has the desire or capability to guard, nurture, and protect them.

Hopeful people have always expected this miracle. Consequently, protest marches, prophetic pronouncements, and prayers are offered to satisfy the rapacious appetites of the predator until the miracle occurs and the wolf lies peacefully with the lamb. But important conceptual changes must take place before models of moral fulfillment and justice can be crafted by societies that incorporate hierarchical and racist assumptions into the very fiber of their societal precepts.

Here we return to Deloria's indictment of liberation theology. He argued that liberation theology lumps diverse and specific people and concerns into one amorphous and dissident community. Energy that could be used to identify and solve specific problems dissipates in debates about philosophy and focus. Accordingly, Deloria wrote, "Liberation theology, then, was an absolute necessity if the establishment was going to continue to control the minds of minorities." He continued, "If a person of a minority group had not invented it, the liberal establishment most certainly would have created it."[10]

Deloria was concerned that the basic tenets of liberation theology are dependent on Western modes of thinking. He was convinced that forging a way out of this maze requires the deconstruction of Western epistemological hierarchies and presumptions about how life should be ordered. His conclusion is stunning. "If there were any serious concern about liberation, we would see thousands of people simply walk away from the vast economic, political, and intellectual machine we call Western civilization and refuse to be enticed to participate in it any longer."[11]

But we are participating in ways that support systems of oppression. The strength to walk away—to make those radical changes and commitments—cannot come until we understand who we are and why we are so deluded by the myths that we help to create.

10. Vine Deloria, Jr., *For This Land: Writings on Religion in America*, ed. James Treat (New York: Routledge, 1999), 100.
11. Ibid., 101.

RACE AND THE COSMOS

The vision is limited

At its inception, liberation rhetoric seemed visionary, and yet it could only describe what members of marginalized communities were not and what they would no longer endure. Very little was said about the big picture. By this, I mean that the discourse did not engage issues such as: Who does God intend for us to be? What is our role in this vast cosmos? How shall we relate to a God who liberates some and not others?[12] Theologian Cynthia L. Rigby reminds us that there is a dialectical tension between modalities of self-help and reliance upon God. If the tension collapses, either the victimized do nothing to liberate themselves as they wait for the transcendent God to deliver them or they take matters into their own hands without reference to divine options.

> In a framework in which God is understood only to liberate, the realization that God has not liberated is extremely dangerous. This is because such realization entails not only that oppressed individuals and communities will suddenly have to work through pain they have repressed; they will also have to do so without the certitude that justice will inevitably be done in the end.[13]

I hear in this argument a refrain that William R. Jones raised in his theodicy challenge to the liberation project. What does it mean to be in relationship with a God who cannot be controlled by human will, but who manifests as the very embodiment of liberty? This is cosmic freedom expressed in ways that we can hardly understand. I consider the tension between the God who acts and the God who doesn't act as creative polarities that hold many possibilities, but the possibilities have not been probed.

Instead, those who championed liberation theology as the ultimate solution and resolution to persistent racial and cultural problems leaped from perspectival constructions to ultimate goals. We claimed the

---

12. Cynthia L. Rigby, "Someone to Blame, Someone to Trust: Divine Power and the Self-Recovery of the Oppressed," in *Power, Powerlessness, and the Divine: New Inquiries in Bible and Theology*, ed. Cynthia L. Rigby (Atlanta: Scholars Press, 1997), 79–102.
13. Ibid., 95.

possibility of a beloved community as a model of multicultural synthesis and a prototype of the *basileia* or Reign of God, but we made this claim without healing the festering generational wounds that racism has inflicted and without public dialogue about the problem of theodicy.

Liberating Liberation:
Some Questions

MOST PEOPLE WOULD agree that liberation is a political, personal, and social concept. However, it is always more than can be described. The following questions need to be addressed if liberation theology is to inform the future.

1. Who is being liberated and from what? Liberationists who are not clear about their goals or their opponents may find themselves confronting the same issues at a later date in a different guise. Moreover, the passage of time allows memories and history to fade. By virtue of generational distance, the progeny of slave holders can claim innocence with regard to inherited positions of power and economic prowess, and the progeny of slaves can use their own personal progress to claim premature victories.

2. After many seasons of oppression, is there an intact "self" left to be free or must we also include the healing of personal and communal trauma as an integral part of the reconstruction of public policy and social change? I take seriously Victor Anderson's call for a test of liberationist goals on the anvil of public policy.

3. Can we institute a pedagogy for the oppressed and oppressors? I am using a term Paulo Freire (1921–1997) used to describe a process that would teach us how to proceed after the dust settles and the movement toward reconciliation is in progress. It is inevitable that, after seasons of oppression, those who once dominated expect the victimized to dust themselves off and start achieving,

competing, and creating a future. The victimized expect all problems to be solved immediately.

Such expectations can never be met. Collective and individual trauma has its consequences. Those subject to it may surrender hope and use material goods to assuage pain, or, in some cases, adopt the ideals and modalities of their tormentors. Tormentors ensnare themselves within the confines of domination, thereby limiting their own potential for liberation.

4. What is the connection between theodicy, radical evil, and our liturgical and discursive reliance upon the God who delivers? Can we maintain historical markers of faith while we attend to the complexity of covenant and the nature of God's care?

5. How can we align social constructs of liberation and justice with emerging cosmic and quantum images? Perhaps solutions to social problems should be linked to our efforts to ascertain the intrinsic aspects of reality.

Some forty-odd years after the Civil Rights movement, we are still seeking solutions to racism. The question is, how shall we dismantle or redeem the systems that have been put in place to perpetuate racism? To date, there have been few answers to this question. There are even fewer options for defining self and society as constructs that do not emerge out of conflict, but out of a full awareness of the realities of the universe and our connections in it.

Something Borrowed:
The Discourses of Law, Sociology, Psychology, and Theology

THE DISCIPLINES OF law, sociology, psychology, and theology provided explanations and coherence for the activist goals and social theories that supported the Civil Rights movement. The marches in the streets, the protests, and the songs needed to be interpreted. Now, we are all conditioned to protests of this type, but, when they began, the body politic wanted to make connections with previously existing discourses. Law, sociology, psychology, and theology were the disciplines that supplied the metaphors, symbols, and analogies that would inform our perspectives on liberation and justice.

Law and freedom

Each discipline would contribute a necessary emphasis and perspective, but law would provide the thematic focus of activism. The challenge was to confront a nation of laws with the unfulfilled spirit of those laws. Law, understood in a Christian perspective, is a process of creating conditions in which sacrificial love, the kind of love personified by Jesus Christ, can take root in society and grow.[14]

The Christian precepts that Martin Luther King, Jr. invoked and the laws that were being enforced by the Supreme Court had different objectives and sources of authority. Yet, in the discourse of liberation, law was understood to be an indispensable partner. It soon became apparent that the conditions for parity and social change required activist courts and new rulings. As the struggles for justice continued, liberation and law became so enmeshed that the discourse of rights began to supplant the language of sacrificial love.

Liberation became synonymous with the mantra of secular culture: "I am free when I have more to spend and the right to spend wherever I choose." The underlying theme was one of radical individualism and complicity with the market forces that were oppressing other members of the two-thirds world.

Today, the limits of rights language have been reached. Rights can't address dysfunction, depression, and low self-esteem. Rights don't have the moxie or the power to uplift whole communities across class lines. Rights are merely recitations of what ought to be in a society of persons who are presumed to be equal.

But when equality becomes a shadow of its ideal formulation, the language of rights is too ponderous to capture meaning. The word "right" becomes as it is used today: a vessel that can be filled by anyone with

---

14. Harold J. Berman, "Law and Love," in *Faith and Order: The Reconciliation of Law and Religion* (Atlanta: Scholars Press, 1993), 313.

private meaning that may run counter to the common good. Rather than expand the vision of liberation, rights discourse displaced communal objectives with issues relevant to individual advancement. This perspective allowed the upward mobility of some, with many left behind.

The failure of the law to undergird the Civil Rights movement with the power to sustain and perpetuate the initiatives led to a pervasive disillusionment. Interestingly enough, the public did not become aware of the vacuity of legal solutions to social problems during civil rights litigation. Rather, the disparities between law and life came to light during public trials that were only peripherally related to issues of liberation.

The O. J. Simpson and Rodney King (1965–2012) trials and recent dismissals of charges against police officers who shoot unarmed POC with impunity are good examples. Whether you believed that O. J. was guilty or not, one thing was clear: majority and minority people viewed the law in completely different ways. A predominantly black and female jury in the O. J. case rejected the "battered woman" prosecution theme and instead acquitted on the basis of "a reasonable doubt." White Simi Valley jurors looked at the Rodney King videotape and concluded that excessive force was not used. A predominantly black jury held otherwise.[15]

Assuming that all jurors attempted to fulfill their duties in accordance with the prevailing law, what accounts for these different outcomes? Legal theorist Anthony E. Cook contends that certain legal standards—"beyond a reasonable doubt," for example—are filtered through the race-based experiences of the jurors.

> "Reasonableness" [is] constructed differently by the different experiences of African-Americans and whites. A history of abuse, pain and suffering inflicted by the police and criminal justice system

---

15. The Rodney King incident occurred on March 3, 1991. On March 15, 1991, four police officers were arraigned on state charges of assault with a deadly weapon. The incident occurred in Los Angeles, but the trial was transferred to Simi Valley in Ventura County. The state trial began on March 5, 1992. On April 29, 1992, a predominately white jury acquitted the officers. A riot took place that lasted six days. Fifty-four people were killed, 2,383 were injured, 13,212 were arrested, and it was estimated that there was $700 million in property damage. On May 2, 1992, the police officers were arraigned on federal civil rights violations. The federal trial began on August 5, 1992, and two defendants were convicted on April 17, 1993.

may have constructed a different standard of "reasonable doubt" for African-American jurors. Similarly, a different set of experiences and understandings of the police, courts and black men, particularly, may have constructed a different standard of what constituted "excessive force" in the minds of Simi Valley jurors.[16]

To construct a reconciled and reconciling community, we must share at least some common visions of justice if the system is to work for all of us. If we don't, as is clearly the case, we must begin public dialogue. This did not happen after the O. J. Simpson and Rodney King trials and it did not happen after the deaths of Trayvon Martin, Sandra Bland, Philando Castile, or the unarmed black men and women killed by the police over the last ten years. The unspoken fear has always been that our differences will finally erupt in violence or catastrophe, and so we avoid the very discussions that could bring us together.

But how does a scientific perspective engage the law? Ted Peters suggests that our lives are infused with an understanding of law as a natural process of the universe.[17] He identifies the laws of nature and God as enhancers of personal freedom to the extent that they "give the individual the opportunity to live with others in a state of peace and cooperation."[18] Law is the community builder, the sustainer of dialectical relationships, and the lynchpin that delineates social and moral boundaries. The turn from this focus to mandated and rights-oriented legal decisions was a crucial shift in perspective.

Sociology: The language of social movements

"Liberation theology has not elaborated social sciences, it has encountered them."[19] Indeed, liberation theology in its incipient stages offered a radical critique of societal and religious structures. In Latin America, it

---

16. Anthony E. Cook, *The Least of These: Race, Law, and Religion in American Culture* (New York: Routledge, 1997), 175.

17. Ted Peters, *God—The World's Future: Systematic Theology for a New Era* (Minneapolis: Fortress, 2000), 281, 282.

18. Ibid., 283.

19. Gustavo Gutiérrez, interview by Paulino Montejo, quoted in "Liberation Theology in the Neoliberal Context," *Latin American Documentation* 25, no. 2 (1994): 17–21.

was a battle cry that resounded throughout the predominantly Catholic continent. In North America, it was a challenge to the exclusionary white church. Both challenges incorporated social and economic initiatives based on new understandings learned from the social sciences. According to Gustavo Gutiérrez,

> A science changes, evolves through hypothesis. The physics of Galileo is not that of Newton, and that of Newton not that of Einstein. And sociology, the social sciences, have the right to change hypotheses according to reality, to interpret poverty in Latin America.[20]

In fact, many liberationists relied on Marxist sociology to make their point and seeded their religious liturgy with the discourse of dependency, exploitation, and class conflict.

> Both liberation theology and Marxism each in its own way is an heir to the Enlightenment, the idea that human beings can, out of their own effort, using their own faculties, particularly rationality, that they can . . . control, dominate and eventually shape the world in their own image.[21]

There are social and economic forces at work that far exceed our delusions of control. All over the world, people are affected by war, natural disasters, and politics, and yet, in terms of structural poverty, things have improved. According to the World Bank, extreme poverty persists in some areas of the world, but has been slowly changing for the better: "About half of the world's countries now have poverty rates below 3 percent, but . . . the world as a whole is not on track to achieve the target of less than 3 percent of the world living in extreme poverty by 2030."[22] According to Gutiérrez,

---

20. Ibid.

21. Manuel Vasquez, "Liberation Theology," interview by Margaret Coffey, *Encounter*, Radio National, the Australian Broadcasting Corporation, July 18, 1999.

22. The World Bank, "Decline of Global Extreme Poverty Continues but Has Slowed: World Bank," press release no. 2019/030/DEC-GPV, September 19, 2018, https://www.worldbank.org/en/news/press-release/2018/09/19/decline-of-global-extreme-poverty-continues-but-has-slowed-world-bank.

the poor achieved "personhood" during the thirty years that elapsed since the beginnings of liberation theology.[23]

Personal esteem was a concomitant benefit of the liberation movements, but the initial focus was on sociological change and the awareness that injustice is incompatible with principles of faith. Whether one ascribes to one political system or another, it is clear that liberation theology calls for Christians to reject hierarchical and capitalistic market forces as an integral part of the movement.

In El Salvador, Archbishop Óscar Romero (1917–1980) was assassinated during Mass. He prioritized the needs of the poor and urged government soldiers to obey God's law instead of human law if they were ordered to kill. The Black Panthers in California and New York began schools and feeding programs to address the issues of body, mind, and spirit.[24]

In most instances, the churches were surprised and uncomfortable with the socially relevant arm of the liberation movements. Some theological leaders were comfortable with separations of church and state that allowed them to avoid difficult social decisions, but the liberation theology movements would not confine their rhetoric to liturgical and eschatological hope. Instead, activists continued to point out the gaps between liturgy and action, praxis and politics.

However, both physics and cosmology speak of interconnections that cannot be defeated by our hatred and abuse. "The self belongs intrinsically to other people through love and even to the cosmos through a unity of being."[25] The social reconciliation that we seek may be part of the order of the life space.

23. Gutiérrez, "Liberation Theology."

24. The two-thirds world embraced liberation as a unique cultural manifestation of God's grace. See the following resources for introductions to liberation discourses in Native American, African American, Hispanic, and Asian contexts: Vine Deloria, Jr., *Red Earth, White Lies: North Americans and the Myth of Scientific Fact* (New York: Scribner, 1995); *Custer Died for Your Sins: An Indian Manifesto* (New York: Macmillan, 1969). James H. Cone, *God of the Oppressed* (Maryknoll, NY: Orbis, 2003); *A Black Theology of Liberation*, rev. ed. (Philadelphia: Lippincott, 2010). Luis G. Pedraja, *Jesus Is My Uncle: Christology from a Hispanic Perspective* (Nashville: Abingdon, 1999). Ada María Isasi-Díaz, *Mujerista Theology* (Maryknoll, NY: Orbis, 1999). Aloysius Pieris, *An Asian Theology of Liberation* (Maryknoll, NY: Orbis, 1988). Kwok Pui-Lan, *Introducing Asian Feminist Theology* (Cleveland: Pilgrim, 2000).

25. Peters, *God*, 282.

Psychology

Issues of esteem pervade the liberation movement. In slogans like "I am somebody," civil rights activist Jesse Jackson spoke to the humiliation and self-hatred that developed during the years of subjugation. The language of overcoming marks liberation theology as a discourse that reflects personal and communal determination. This stance toward the world has very definite psychological contours. When unworthiness crystallizes as an internal reality, it is difficult to unseat it. Liberation theology could not assuage this pain.

Parker Palmer makes the connection between a loss of connection to self and the problems of relating to others and the life space. In a statement that is worth quoting in full, he says,

> When you have lost the capacity, as many in this world have, to connect with the deepest parts of yourself, then you're simply living life on the level of role, function, image, status. Whether that's living life on the level of the inflated ego or the deflated ego doesn't make much difference. It's still not the real you.[26]

When we are not authentically in touch with self, we cannot respond in any meaningful or responsible way to society. Oppressor and victim modalities are examples of the false categories of inflated and deflated egos that do not represent the real person.

Theologian Kathryn Tanner presents a similar idea in her book *The Politics of God,* in which she says that it is idolatrous to esteem self above others, but it is equally idolatrous to harbor and nurture low self-esteem. Both extremes and the myriad possibilities that range between them are denigrations of God's image.[27] Tanner proposes a non-idolatrous self-esteem that more accurately reflects divine intent and human potential. A connection to the deepest parts of the self precedes the turn to "others."

Both self and society are matters within our grasp. Those matters beyond our reach, such as the nature of reality, the attributes of God,

26. Parker Palmer, "Spiritual Formation and Social Change," in *Fugitive Faith: Interviews by Benjamin Webb* (Maryknoll, NY: Orbis, 1998), 57.
27. Tanner, *The Politics of God.*

and the logarithm of the universe, require only our intense curiosity and imaginative seeking. The contribution that science makes to our understanding of psychology is addressed in chapter 8.

The discussion about quantum processes in psychology points to the possibility that human consciousness may originate in the brain but have a metaphysical reach that extends beyond the physical. This raises questions as to the locus of wholeness and well-being and the interconnections of varied life forces.

Theology

Liberation theology borrowed symbols and metaphors from Holy Scripture that focused on deliverance and a God who favors the poor. It became the story of all people displaced from one land or one reality to another. If God was on the side of the oppressed, the particularities of oppression could not override the cosmic determinations of a universe set in motion by divine forces that were wedded to justice.

The prophets proclaimed the idea, the Hebrews lived through the amazing reality, and sacred texts attested to the possibilities. When the narratives of deliverance finally moved people from prayer and hymn to praxis and action, the liberation movements were in full swing. However, they did not take into account the theodicy questions posed by William R. Jones, who argued that God is the sum of God's acts. The question is one of God's character and ours, and where the responsibility lies for repetitive historical abuses.

Process theology does not resolve these issues, but points in the direction of shared human/divine responsibility. The elements of process thought that are important to this discussion include the belief that the future is genuinely open, that God must constantly adjust to meet changing circumstances, and that all of reality, including God, is energy.[28]

For process theologians, the call to liberation is clear. God has a vision of universal dignity and equality.[29] However, human social and historical

---

28. William Stegall, "A Guide to A. N. Whitehead's *Understanding of God and the Universe*," *Creative Transformation,* Center for Process Studies (Spring 1995).

29. C. Robert Mesle, *Process Theology: A Basic Introduction* (St. Louis: Chalice, 1993), 85–90. See also Bruce G. Epperly, *Process Theology: A Guide for the Perplexed*

contexts garble the message, concluding that God supports their inclinations toward dominance and oppression. Meanwhile, God continually struggles to draw humankind toward a liberative vision. God's power is persuasive, an attribute that does not match our depictions of God as male warrior.

It is quite a quantum leap to move from anthropomorphic childhood images to the process depiction of God as pure energy, an energy that invigorates and sustains the matrix of life. "God is the web, the energy, the space, the light—not captured in them . . . but revealed, in that singular vast net of relationship that animates everything that is."[30] If God is embedded in every human quantum and cosmological event, oppression takes on a brazen and defiant stance that opposes the divine within everything.[31]

On one level, we have kinship and genetic linkages with "life that is perishing." Nevertheless, "we are also made in the image and likeness of Another, whose code is transcendent."[32] In every human cell, there seems to be memory of the Transcendent One, even when we are living somnambulant lives. The joy of this theological revelation is that it offers hope and prods human curiosity toward the limits of its ability to know.

We get hints of meaning from the events and responses that occur in space and on quantum levels. However, faith attestations seldom incorporate the ideas from science that shed new light on traditional religious principles. I am imagining a Christian confession of faith that could include the attestation that Christ is a cosmic companion whose body is a hologram of divine and human possibilities that erupts out of a quantum singularity to offer a redemption that transcends infinity.

David S. Toolan (1935–2002) offered a communion liturgy that startles and refreshes with its mixed entreaty of scientific and faith discourses. He referred to this perspective as "new music in the world."

(New York: T & T Clark, 2011).

30. Barbara Brown Taylor, *The Luminous Web: Essays on Science and Religion* (Cambridge, MA: Cowley, 2000), 74.

31. Richard Rohr, *The Universal Christ: How a Forgotten Reality Can Change Everything We See, Hope For, and Believe* (New York: Convergent, 2019).

32. Carol Zaleski, "In Defense of Immortality," *First Things* 105 (August–September 2000): 37.

Swallow this, Jesus effectively declares, I am God's promise for the elements, the exemplary inside of nature, its secret wish fulfilled. Assume my role. Swallow me and you will have taken in what God imagines for matter—that it be spirited and at peace.[33]

Toolan reminded us that something amazing happens at theological events like the Last Supper.

No theatrics, no magic, simply the highly charged, polyvalent symbolics of what a human body can contain and dispense. Two great movements converge in what Jesus shows us here—the everlasting desire of cosmic dust to mean something great and God's promise that it shall be so.[34]

Why not allow liturgy to awaken us to the possibilities of the universe and our unique stance as conscious and self-aware beings? Why not consider a God who interacts in eleven dimensions in ways that can synthesize indigenous practices and mainstream theological discourse with the languages of the universe? The God who interacts in human history but is beyond human reach may surprise us with divine and secular serenades of impermanence and potential rather than the certitude and security that we seek.

Summary

THE FOUNDATIONS OF liberation discourse have lost their ability to lead a troubled nation toward moral flourishing. This ultimate and cataclysmic loss can be described as a palpable and absorbing silence that not only fails to respond to crying needs, but mutes dissent to such a point that the one who cries out cannot even discern the source of the howl.

The cry is not for reconciliation. The very concept of reconciliation assumes that, despite unresolved issues, it is time to move on for the

33. David S. Toolan, "Praying in a Post-Einsteinian Universe," *Cross Currents* 46, no. 4 (Winter 1996–1997), 437–470, http://www.crosscurrents.org/toolan.html.

34. Ibid.

greater good. As a nation, we have tried, without success and without a truth and reconciliation commission, to move on. However, rhetorical yokes continue to ensnare us in cycles of blaming and distrust.

The liberation theology project must move its focus beyond protest to human fulfillment. It must also admit that integration is not the ultimate goal and that liberation can't be socially or legally engineered. Although justice must be enacted in concrete ways, I agree with Václav Havel (1936–2011) that liberation is seeded in transcendence. Havel said that the key to the human journey and the enigma of the universe as well as our responsibility to one another lies in "what transcends humanity, in what stands above it."[35] He suggested that liberation is an awareness of connections to a reality "beyond our reach, a higher intention that is the source of all things, a higher memory recording everything, a higher authority to which we are all accountable in one way or another."[36]

Perhaps it was the awareness of the violation of those connections that caused Archbishop Desmond Tutu to weep during the Truth and Reconciliation Commission hearings. He laid his head on a table made of vibrating quantum elements as he wept in deep, sonorous tones that reached beyond the galaxies and into the consciousness of a pathologically dry-eyed people. When he wept, the universe wept with him about a truth that we are unable to face.

There are no beasts to slay. We are the fire-breathing principalities and powers, the seers and prophets, the giants and faith-filled vanquishers. The truth is both wave and particle; the solution is in the singularity of individual choice and shared commitments.

---

35. Václav Havel, "A Sense of the Transcendent," talk at the National Press Club, Canberra, Australia, March 29, 1995; published in *Cross Currents* 47, no. 3 (Fall 1997).
   36. Ibid.

three

:::

We may consider science and religion as two windows
through which we look at the world.
The world is one and the same.
But what we see through those windows is different. . . .
Science has to do with the expansion of galaxies and movement
of the continents and the origin of organisms and adaptations.
Religion has to do with our relationship to our creator and to each other,
with the purpose and meaning of life,
with moral values that govern our lives.
So, they deal with different subjects so [there is] no need
to contradict each other.

—Francisco Ayala,
2010 Templeton Award Winner

:::

Who can walk into unknown woods
and head directly for the other side?
Wandering for a spell sometimes makes the journey
even more exciting.

—Vine Deloria, Jr.,
The Metaphysics of Modern Existence

:::

Science, Theology, and Culture:
The Perils and Possibilities of Shared Discourses

The whole of science is nothing more than a refinement of everyday thinking.
—Albert Einstein, *Physics and Reality*

Everything is physics and math.
—Katherine Johnson, *Hidden Figures*

I MAGINE THAT YOU are in a circus tent filled with cheering crowds, delighted children, and cotton candy. With a musical flourish and a drum roll, spotlights focus on two platforms that are perched high above your head. Although it is difficult to see, you know that a thin wire connects the platforms and allows high-wire artists to walk from one perch to another. As you watch this spectacle, you understand that, although these suspenseful journeys are fraught with danger and uncertainty, it would be ludicrous to suggest a more substantial crossing device. This is not the place to build a two-lane highway or thicker balance beam. The wire is what it is. In the stated situation, danger and intrigue are inherent to the crossings.

Crossings between science and theology can be just as perilous. Experts in both fields fear the trivialization of their findings and beliefs as a result of careless appropriations in interdisciplinary contexts or facile and ill-fitting analogies borrowed from one field and applied in another.[1] In fact, some people contend that the high-wire artists who are attempting to bridge the conflicts between theology and science have earned the scorn of both camps.

Albert Einstein (1879–1955) did not let this debate escape his attention. He stated, "The present fashion of applying the axioms of physical science to human life is not only entirely a mistake but has also something reprehensible in it."[2] Yet he is also quoted as saying, "Reality is the real business of physics." It is clear that when Einstein talks about "reality," he is not referring to changing diapers or buying toothpaste.

Instead, Einstein is talking about a method of inquiry and analysis that is not generally accessible or applicable to daily life. One wonders how he can disdain the use of the physical sciences to explicate the everyday world, when the physical sciences are not divorced from the mundane. The connections may not be visible, but they are there.

It is unfortunate when scientists separate themselves and their findings from the culture that is the source of their inspiration. The consequence is that ordinary folks expect to be excluded from scientific conversations. They don't believe that they have the technical skills to understand the concepts and, for the most part, they believe that science is more congruent with experimentation and mathematical constructs than with the problems and pleasures that define their lives.

They have reached similar conclusions about theology and recognize the fact that theology tends to focus its academic curiosity about God far from the messy and down-to-earth issues that concern ordinary people. Whether we admit it or not, the work of physicists, cosmologists, theologians, and high-wire artists seems esoteric when compared to the demands of everyday life.

For ethnic communities, the connection between daily life, theology, and science is even more tenuous. Given a social context that requires

---

1. Max Planck, *Where Is Science Going?* (New York: Norton, 1932), 209, cited in Ken Wilber, *Quantum Questions: Mystical Writings of the World's Greatest Physicists* (Boulder, CO: Shambhala, 1984), 27.

2. Albert Einstein, as cited by Planck in Wilber, *Quantum Questions*, 3.

ongoing skirmishes with injustice, poverty, personal relationships, and group dynamics, most don't know what to say or do about quarks, theodicy, gluons, black holes, grace, and vibrating superstrings. Yet, the cultural connections are beginning to emerge.

This chapter probes the intersections of theology, science, and culture, and further engages the barriers of mistrust that have been erected. At this point, I will remind the reader that the cultural appropriations proposed in this book are not the usual subject of debates about science and religion. Discussions of physics, cosmology, and religion tend to focus on God's existence or nonexistence, the connection between scientific discoveries about cosmic origins and human destiny, and the relationship between quantum events and immortality.

These conversations, though important, tend to be captive to modernist assumptions and, until recently, did not include the perspectives of the two-thirds world in any meaningful way.[3] I will only briefly discuss the science and religion debate, as there are many excellent volumes that delineate the issues.[4] Martin Luther King, Jr. also commented on the purported conflict between the two disciplines.

> There may be a conflict between soft-minded religionists and tough-minded scientists, but not between science and religion. . . . Science investigates; religion interprets. Science gives . . . knowledge that is power; religion gives . . . wisdom that is control. . . . The two are not rivals. They are complementary. Science keeps religion from sinking into the valley of crippling irrationalism and paralyzing obscurantism. Religion prevents science from falling into the marsh of obsolete materialism and moral nihilism.[5]

3. I am happy to report that change is on the way. The Center for Theology and the Natural Sciences, located in Berkeley, California, hosted conferences focusing on African, Native American, and Asian perspectives on science and religion in the years 2001–2002. Other organizations have followed their example.

4. Among these are Ian G. Barbour, *Religion in an Age of Science: The Gifford Lectures, Vol. 1* (San Francisco: HarperSanFrancisco, 1990); John F. Haught, *Science and Religion: From Conflict to Conversation* (Mahwah, NJ: Paulist, 1995); and William Grassie, *The New Sciences of Religion: Exploring Spirituality from the Outside In and Bottom Up* (New York: Metanexus Imprints, 2019).

5. Martin Luther King, Jr., *Strength to Love* (New York: Harper & Row, 1958), 3.

King seemed to be moving toward the idea of consonance rather than conflict between science and religion. Most science and religion discussions attempt to categorize points of agreement and dissonance through the use of typologies. For a discussion of typologies, I find Ian Barbour's book *When Science Meets Religion: Enemies, Strangers, or Partners?* very useful.

Barbour explores intersections of science and religion through a discussion of conflict, independence, dialogue, and integration. He suggests that conflict between science and religion most often occurs when scientific materialism and biblical literalism control the conversation. Scientific materialism assumes that matter is the quintessential element of reality and that "the scientific method is the only reliable path to knowledge."[6]

The independence approach to science and religion assumes a categorization of the life space that is not supported by either discipline. We do not live in a world that separates life energies. As quantum physics is beginning to unveil, assumed separations often result from a lack of understanding of underlying connections. Barbour's dialogue category influences this particular study and suggests that "methodological and conceptual parallels" between the disciplines of theology and science have the potential to enlighten both.[7] The final category, integration, can be problematic if the very real distinctions and disagreements between theology and science are artificially minimized.

The languages used to describe the pursuit of knowledge in each field seem to be the biggest impediment to enriching interdisciplinary exchanges. Math and liturgy seem to have nothing to do with one another, yet each discourse reaches its limit and must ultimately look beyond rhetorical boundaries to describe the world.

Epistemological differences need not be solved; they can be bridged through the use of metaphors, symbols, and analogies. This book assumes that the quest for justice is a social, theological, and scientific construct, and, by that, I mean that liberation must take the entire life space (including science) into account.

---

6. Ian G. Barbour, *When Science Meets Religion: Enemies, Strangers, or Partners?* (New York: HarperOne, 2000), 11.

7. Ibid., 38.

Science and Religion:
A Brief History

FROM THE EARLIEST of times, science and religion shared a curiosity about the ways of the world. In diverse cultures, curious people looked up and wondered about the starry firmament. Both religions and science told stories about the origins of the universe and humankind. "The story of the modern scientific worldview begins with how we came to 'know' the earth moves and not the sun."[8] Greek astronomer Aristarchus of Samos (c. 310–c. 230 BC) determined that the earth orbits around the sun rather than the reverse, but was ignored. He was not the first. People in indigenous cultures made similar observations, but many encoded the information in oral repositories that died with their narrators.

The idea of earth's centrality in the universe is deeply rooted in the theological premise that God created and focused divine attention on the earth. Such presumptions are not easily displaced. Aristotle (384–322 BC) agreed on the earth-centered model, as did Ptolemy (c. 100–c. 170 AD) and St. Thomas Aquinas (1225–1274).[9] A change came during the Renaissance, when Nicholas Copernicus (1473–1543), a Polish priest and astronomer, suggested that the sun rather than the earth might be the center of the universe.[10] He was wise enough to realize that the reaction of the church might affect his life span, so he waited until he was dying to reveal his findings.[11]

It was not that the church was anti-science; its primary objection was to the theological conclusions being deduced from scientific observations. The ecclesial response to any variation from the main theme that emphasized God's order and human centrality was calamitous. People who disagreed with the flat earth theory or the dogma of the church

---

8. Bruce Gregory, *Inventing Reality: Physics as Language* (New York: John Wiley & Sons, 1988), 7.

9. Fred Alan Wolf, *Taking the Quantum Leap: The New Physics for Non-Scientists* (New York: Harper & Row, 1989), 28.

10. Tilby, *Soul*, 40.

11. Taylor, *Luminous Web*, 51. It is interesting to note that Copernicus' discoveries coincided with the European landings in the Americas and the Spanish conquest of Mexico. His era also overlaps with Martin Luther (1483–1546), Niccolò Machiavelli (1469–1527), Thomas More (1478–1535), and St. Ignatius of Loyola (1491–1556).

regarding the divinity/humanity of Jesus were labeled heretics. To be labeled a heretic meant that some dire punishment such as burning or quartering was inevitable.

Those who were struggling to maintain the status quo felt that they had to destroy a human body to eliminate an idea. It was an irrational response, since ideas can survive without a human host. Although ideas by their very nature require articulation, they can speak through text as well as the human voice. Even if the texts are destroyed, deep-seated memories will prod subsequent generations to revisit the concepts. If all else fails, young men and women will see visions, and old men and women will dream dreams (Acts 2:17). Killing the thinker can't kill the thought. This is small comfort, however, to those who paid the ultimate price for their questions and suppositions.

Despite the draconian responses of the church to the findings of curious men and women who insisted on studying the skies, science continued to provoke new ideas about the nature of the universe. In the nineteenth century, impermeable divisions soon separated religion and science. The artifacts of those divisions remain with us today. Religion would reign over the spiritual, poetic, and metaphoric truths, while the sciences would focus on verifiable facts.[12] Today, religion still claims a stake in truth that requires faith, while science relies on "objective" claims and the ability to test its precepts in repeatable experiments. In the extreme, both offer diminished and reduced life descriptions that present only a shadow of reality. Despite efforts to bring the disciplines back into conversation, each tells a different story about life, death, and human origins.

Classical Physics and Cosmology

Galileo galilei (1564–1642), an Italian astronomer, confirmed Copernicus' observations and built a telescope that magnified the heavens thirty times.[13] According to a popular story, his observations about the properties of moving objects began in church. During a particularly

12. Tilby, *Soul*, 134.
13. Ibid., 41.

boring sermon, Galileo began to note the direction and motion of a chandelier that was swinging like a pendulum in the wind coming from an open door. Timing the beats with the rate of his pulse, he noticed that the rate was the same for every sixty beats. He had discovered a law of motion that would make the invention of clocks possible.[14]

For his scientific probes of the universe, Galileo was brought before the Inquisition, forced to recant, and placed under house arrest for the remainder of his life.[15] It was an unhappy but better option than the immolation that ended Giordano Bruno's curiosity. Bruno (1548–1600) said that there was a vast universe that included other planetary systems.

Knowledge increased with the discoveries of Johannes Kepler (1571–1630), a German Lutheran. Kepler used mathematics to devise laws of celestial motion and explained the movement of planets as elliptical rather than circular orbits, thereby providing a foundation for Isaac Newton's laws of motion.

The Newtonian age coincides with the beginning of the Enlightenment era. Although the Enlightenment is synonymous with the rise of secularism and reason, Newton (1642–1727) did not approach science with the intent to displace religion. He was a religious man who believed that he was uncovering God's design, a design that was mechanistic in a clockwork universe. To reach his conclusions, Newton incorporated the work of Galileo and Kepler into his own formulations about the laws of gravity and motion.

When I speak of laws, I am referring to fundamental principles that evince a picture of the world. Newton's laws of motion postulated that objects rest or move in a continuous way unless they are intercepted or impacted by another force, and that every action has an equal and opposite reaction.[16]

Newton also argued that when a force intercepts an object, "the rate of change in the momentum of a moving body relates to and is in the same direction as the force that moves it."[17] In conjunction with these

---

14. Wolf, *Taking the Quantum Leap*, 33.

15. Ibid., 33–37.

16. Gary Zukav, *The Dancing Wu Li Masters: An Overview of the New Physics* (New York: Bantam, 1979), 21.

17. Tilby, *Soul*, 43.

findings, Newton found that gravity was the cohesive force that affected planetary motion and pulled falling objects toward the earth. But he was confounded, even as he made the discovery, and his question was, "How can one body act upon another at a distance?"[18] Soon quantum physics would ask the same question in a different way.

Newton found that "everything moves. Everything attracts everything else."[19] In short, he was unveiling a universe in motion. Newton's findings are still applicable for making large-scale determinations. In fact, the American space program still relies on those basic formulations to determine where and when spaceships will dock with stations and land upon return. It is in the subatomic world where the theories reach their limit.

To Newton, the universe resembled a well-oiled machine. Even today, his mechanistic view of the cosmos fits easily within human desires for order and predictability. "Since Newton applied this mechanical interpretation of nature to all forms of existence, he formulated the principles of mechanical science into a cosmology."[20]

To assert that Newton's theories reached beyond science to culture is to recognize the impact of a theory of the world that was congruent with cultural inclinations toward dominance and oppression. Newton's theories of a knowable and orderly universe took hold in ways that seemed to confirm the social hierarchies that were solidifying in the world. Science supported a hierarchy with God at the top and certain human beings in a superior position to others. Given such a rigid schema, dominance over the earth and "lesser" societies seemed inevitable.

> The Newtonian paradigm is individualistic from beginning to end. Each bit of matter was thought to be separate, autonomous, independent and self-contained. Reality did not contain internal relatedness. Rather, each form of reality was highly individualized and mechanized, meaning that it functioned based on absolute spacetime.[21]

18. Zukav, *Dancing Wu Li*, 23.
19. Tilby, *Soul*, 44.
20. Young, *Hope in Process*, 16.
21. Ibid., 22.

RACE AND THE COSMOS

If the story that was coming from science was to be believed, the world was a predictable, predetermined, and hierarchical space. These presumptions laid the groundwork for cultural violations that continue to the present day. But the more devastating effect may not have been the presumption of interhuman domination, but the spiritual alienation that followed.

In many ways, a mechanistic universe left humankind theologically isolated from the most basic human-divine connections. Once the Newtonian cosmos was set in motion, it did not require the intervention or care of God. As David S. Toolan noted, "An inert, mechanistic landscape is not semiotic, a set of numinous signs, as the medieval material world had been.... All analogy or kinship of being is broken—and we are effectively shut out (or shut up within our own bag of skin)."[22]

Being shut up within a personal bag of skin is the beginning of the delusion of radical independence from others and God. From a cultural perspective, the Newtonian world order supported institutional and social hierarchies as well as personal perceptions of radical autonomy until the new cosmologies challenged every assumption.

What's New about the New Physics and Cosmology?

PRIOR TO THE DISCOVERY of the electron in 1897 by Joseph John Thomson (1856–1940), it was presumed that the atom was the smallest division of matter. The search for the smallest element of matter would lead to the unveiling of a quantum world. At the same time, scientists were contemplating the properties of light and Einstein's theories of general and special relativity were on the horizon. James Clerk Maxwell (1831–1879) discovered the laws of electromagnetic fields and determined that light was a moving electromagnetic wave.

In the 1900s, German physicist Max Planck (1858–1947) determined that energy traveled in small jumps (quanta). His findings were related to the study of "black body radiation." Scientists knew, in accordance with the laws of classical physics, that heated objects like black iron changed color when heated. They calculated the color that should be reached

22. Toolan, "Praying," 5.

when particles were moving rapidly during the heating process and determined that black bodies, when heated, should glow bright blue. Instead, they glowed red.

Planck solved the problem using the research of Heinrich Rubens (1865–1922) as a basis. The key to his analysis was understanding that light traveled in energy transfers described as "discrete packets" rather than waves.[23] Einstein later used this theory to explain the photoelectronic effect and the movement of light in quanta packets called photons. Even though scientists wanted definitive answers to their questions about the properties of light, they were left with a description of light as particle and wave.

The word "quantum" means quantity or amount. Quantum theory says that nature comes in packets or quanta. The properties of quanta are very strange indeed. "One could never say for sure whether they were particles or waves of energy, whether they could be said to exist at definite times and places or whether they tended to exist as probability waves."[24]

Welcome to the world of quantum physics, the study of subatomic particles and the reality structures that govern their attributes. At the turn of the twentieth century, physicists awakened to a world that was indeterminate, in much the same way as theologians six decades later would awaken to the fact that foundational elements of Christian theology were skewed in favor of the oppressed. Our fixed perspectives of reality would never be the same.

In quantum physics, we are being handed probability rather than stasis, connections that transcend the limits of human embodiment and a life space that vibrates and hums with intelligence. These tools can tear down the false constructs that erected and supported racism. Such upheavals, though not intended to change the life space, cannot avoid that outcome.

Christian theology tells another story, of chosenness and selection, for the glory of God. The idea of chosenness can be problematic in cultural contexts when viewed through the lens of radical individualism. In Western contexts, society is organized so that only one team can win, only one runner can break the tape. All else is loss. In fact, the universe may be

23. Michio Kaku and Jennifer Thompson, *Beyond Einstein: The Cosmic Quest for the Theory of the Universe* (New York: Anchor, 1995), 38, 39.
24. O'Murchu, *Quantum Theology*, 27.

more reflective of the perspectives of indigenous communities who often foster a win/win social environment, with losses integrated as normative and balancing events. If the universe is as interconnected as some suppose, its survival can't be separated from ours.

The Cultural Connection

WHAT DO WE MEAN when we speak of culture? Some anthropologists believe that "culture in essence . . . constitutes the shared survival strategies of a group of people."[25] Others focus on key values passed down between generations. Kenyan scholar Joshua J. Akong'a (1949–2017) suggested that culture is a repository of shared meaning; it is a communal and language-based experience that can't be relegated to individual practices.

Moreover, culture is both cumulative and organic as it reflects the influences of varied human activities.[26] Science contributes to culture just as much as any other human endeavor, and those contributions are not limited to technology and medical science. Indeed, "science shapes human consciousness, is culturally formative; it invariably communicates itself by—or is transformed into—the kind of tacit cultural myths by which we live."[27]

The connections between science, theology, and culture seem to be artificial because of the historical failure to incorporate the scientific perspectives of indigenous and ethnic cultures into mainstream science. One need only read the history of science to note the omissions. Where are the interests, perspectives, and findings of women, and ethnic and indigenous people?

Even now, there is the presumption that European questions and perspectives in science are normative. One clear example of this continuing presumption is that researchers rarely go any further than the Mediterranean

25. Michael C. Howard and Patrick C. McKim, *Contemporary Cultural Anthropology* (Boston: Little, Brown, 1983), 5.

26. Joshua J. Akong'a, "Basic Concepts of Culture," presented at African Culture, Modern Science, and Religious Thought Conference, University of Ilorin, Nigeria, October 19–24, 2001, in collaboration with the Center for Theology and the Natural Sciences, Berkeley, California.

27. Toolan, "Praying," 3.

to study the indigenous origins of scientific thought. In fact, it is not unusual for those who analyze both the progression of classical physics and the evolution of theology to begin with the Greeks.

Theologian Robert E. Hood (1936–1994), in his book *Must God Remain Greek? Afro Cultures and God-Talk*, made the point that Eurocentric hegemonies often rely on Greco-Roman sources as a historical foundation while deleting or ignoring other indigenous wisdom that predated both cultures. Hood argued that the reason for these selective recitations of history is rooted in the desire for power. To determine that everything worthwhile comes from Eurocentric cultures shapes the future in ways that deny power to all others. To be descended from the presumed architects of culture and civilization bequeaths the right to determine which groups stand outside the circle of intellect and rationality. Hood noted that these presumptions inevitably result in a proliferation of hierarchies and paternalism toward "primitive cultures."[28]

Yet all of humanity's ancestors were primitive participants in tribal units at one point in history or another, and curiosity about the world neither begins nor ends with Europe or the West. As the world becomes more and more connected, we are learning that indigenous cultures of Africa, Asia, and the Americas intuited, observed, and narratively constructed a relationship to the universe and to the divine.

Some indigenous observations have withstood the passage of time and the increase in human knowledge; other songs and stories have been lost or reflect the permeable boundaries between the physical world and the dream or vision states. In the area of race relations, both theology and science have failed us. History reminds us that theologians found biblical warrant for the oppression of African slaves and justification for the perpetuation of the institution of slavery. Conversion efforts had multiple aims. It was presumed by slave masters that the Christian faith would encourage slaves to acquiesce and accept their fate. The promise of freedom in the "by and by" relieved owners of the need to redress grievous human rights violations in the "here and now."

Science has a similar history of complicity with the forces of domination. In fact, those who wanted proof of inferiority turned to scientists

28. Robert E. Hood, *Must God Remain Greek? Afro Cultures and God-Talk* (Minneapolis: Fortress, 1990), 3.

to make their cases. It was pseudoscience and its analogies that situated African Americans somewhere between animals and human beings. In 1799, English physician Charles White (1728–1813) concluded that blacks were a separate species. Moreover, he argued that "the superior memory some blacks displayed . . . was an ability shared by a number of domestic animals, like the horse and the dog."[29]

Physician Samuel Cartwright (1793–1863), chairman of the Medical Association of Louisiana, determined that it was not a desire for freedom that drove slaves to escape but the mental disease of "drapetomania." Cartwright suggested that treating slaves as children could cure the malady. Owners were urged to show kindness and paternalism and to punish and whip severely to induce a submissive attitude.[30] "Samuel Stanhope Smith [1751–1819], president of the College of New Jersey (later Princeton), hoped that American blacks, in a climate more suited to Caucasian temperaments, would soon turn white."[31]

These stories reflect the times and mindset of men and women ensconced in an era of imperialism. They are included here to make the point that neither science nor theology is immune from virulent strains of social injustice. In fact, eugenics, social Darwinism, ethnic cleansing, and the slaughter of Native American, Jewish, and African communities indicate the tendency for science and theology to mirror the aberrations of the culture. During the nineteenth century, theology focused on the curse of Ham as justification for Africans' presumed alienation from God and white society, while scientific theories of inferiority focused on monogenetic and polygenetic theories.

Monogenism argued that all human beings were descendants of Adam and Eve but that some had degenerated more than others. Polygenism offered separate creations and ancestral parents for each "race." Louis Agassiz (1807–1873), Swiss-born naturalist and Harvard scholar, was a polygenist whose work formed the foundation for pseudoscientific

29. Charles White, *An Account of the Regular Gradation in Man and in Different Animals and Vegetables; and from the Former to the Latter* (London: C. Dilly, 1799), 94–95; also quoted in William H. Tucker, *The Science and Politics of Racial Research* (Champaign, IL: University of Illinois Press, 1993), 11.

30. Samuel Cartwright, "Dr. Cartwright on the Caucasians and the Africans," *DeBow's Review* 25:1 (July 1858), 45–56.

31. Gould, "American Polygeny," 184.

proofs of inferiority. He is quoted as saying, "What unhappiness for the white race—to have tied their existence so closely with the Negroes in certain countries! God preserve us from such contact."[32] Agassiz developed the philosophical theories that supported ideas of inferiority while Dr. Samuel Morton (1799–1851) supported Agassiz's findings with craniology studies.

Morton measured the skull capacity of men and women with mustard seeds and steel pellets. His findings spawned a discourse of immutable inadequacies so pervasive that even W. E. B. Du Bois found it difficult to resist its assumptions. At one point, Du Bois offered to measure the heads of one thousand students at the Hampton Institute in Atlanta to refute the theory of their inferiority.[33] The measurements could not defuse the issue as it is difficult to deconstruct a racist premise that is supported by purportedly neutral and objective "scientific facts."

It is important to note that the effort to document the inferiority of racial/ethnic groups was not exclusively aimed at African Americans. To the contrary, the influx of European immigrants also triggered xenophobic responses and the effort to document objective reasons for collective fear and aversion.[34]

In the medical arena, stories abound of abuse and mythology. The Tuskegee syphilis experiment is perhaps the most heinous instance of breached medical ethics in recent history. The event took place from 1932 to 1972, when the United States government, through a local health facility, promised poor African American men treatment for "bad blood" or syphilis. Instead, the men were observed for forty years while the disease progressed. When penicillin became available, they were denied treatment.

When the story became public on July 5, 1972, it exposed the complicity of public health officials, government workers, and some African American doctors and nurses in Macon County, Alabama. The men and

---

32. Ibid., 95.

33. Nancy Leys Stepan and Sander L. Gilman, "Appropriating the Idioms of Science: The Rejection of Scientific Racism," in *The Racial Economy of Science: Toward a Democratic Future*, ed. Sandra Harding (Bloomington, IN: Indiana University Press, 1993), 184.

34. Ibid.

their families filed a class-action lawsuit and received a $10 million out-of-court settlement.[35] In 1977, President Clinton apologized.

Most of us would rather forget these ignominious moments in history. The problem with forgetting is that the results are still with us. Acts may cease but effects persist. If, as physicists assert, time is not linear, but relative, then artifacts of pseudo-sciences that were encoded in the culture continue to affect the present and the future. The belief that people of color are intrinsically inferior still sustains environmental racism and the unequal allotment of civic resources in ethnic communities. The images and rhetoric coming from physics and cosmology may unsettle these myths with concepts of power and vibrancy. Now, this story must be told in the same places where stories of domination once prevailed.

Summary

I HAVE SEEN high-wire performers grasping a long pole to give them a wider center of gravity. They move swiftly, relying on nets below. For most members of two-thirds-world communities, the act of self-definition can be a daunting high-wire act between multiple platforms of self-esteem, survival modalities, and toxic assimilations.

While the languages of science are neither salvific nor the final answer to issues of identity and racism in North America, they do increase the options for people captive to the nightmare of never-ending "overcoming" and imposed definitions of selfhood. As Deloria noted, "Wandering for a spell sometimes makes the journey even more exciting" and perhaps more interesting, but for those who have been wandering toward justice since they arrived on Western shores, it is time to arrive.[36]

---

35. James H. Jones, *Bad Blood: The Tuskegee Syphilis Experiment* (New York: Free Press, 1993), 199. See also Emilie M. Townes' discussion in *Breaking the Fine Rain of Death: African American Health Issues and a Womanist Ethic of Care* (New York: Continuum, 1998), 88–100 and Harriet A. Washington, *Medical Apartheid: The Dark History of Medical Experimentation on Black Americans from Colonial Times to the Present* (New York: Random House, 2006).

36. Vine Deloria, Jr., *The Metaphysics of Modern Existence* (San Francisco: Harper & Row, 1979), xii.

The next chapter returns us to indigenous fires around the world, where scientific knowledge was dispensed as pragmatic wisdom in song and chant. Recent discoveries of prehistoric symbols, drawings, and narrative recollections document the cosmological observations of the two-thirds world.

four

My Grandfather Was a Quantum Physicist

I can see him now
smiling
in full dance regalia
in front of the roundhouse
on a sunny afternoon

Scientists have finally discovered
that the intimate details
of our lives
are influenced by things
beyond the stars
and beyond time

My grandfather knew this

—Duane Big Eagle,
Songs from This Earth on Turtle's Back

:::

I pointed out to you the stars (and the moon)
and all you saw was the tip of my finger.

—Sukuma proverb,
Tanzania

:::

⠿ *4* ⠿

"Dem as Could Fly Home":
Indigenous Wisdom and Science

We may know immeasurably more about the universe than our ancestors did, and yet, it increasingly seems they knew something more essential about it than we do, something that escapes us. . . . Transcendence [is] the only real alternative to extinction.

—Václav Havel,
"The Need for Transcendence in the Postmodern World"

"I say when we came to Africa, we could fly. You heard me. We could fly. . . . But we ate too much salt. Can't mess with too much salt cause it throws things out of proper balance. If you scientific, you know that. . . . And when the forces were all in balance, we were at the center of the field. The electro mag-net-tic [sic] field. . . . Gravity? Don't be tellin me about no some such gravity. That aint nuthin. We could fly. I'm tellin you some-thing and I hope you listening. We could fly."

—Ma Hudson, in Toni Cade Bambara,
The Sea Birds Are Still Alive

VÁCLAV HAVEL and Toni Cade Bambara (1939–1995) came from vastly different contexts, yet they agree: To survive on this planet, you have to know how to fly. You have to be able to soar above the situations, boredom, and muck of daily life. Flying as transcendence can be accomplished in any number of ways; the method of transport is not nearly as important as the effect on spirit and soul. What is important is that, inevitably, those who fly by means of creative practices, music, dream states, scientific inquiry, or stories tend to remember their primal connections to cosmic reality. The title of this chapter is taken from the slave narrative of Phyllis Green, who said, "Muh ma tell me many times bout a man and his wife wut could wuk cunjuh. Anytime dey want tuh dey would fly back tuh Africa and den come back agen to duh plantation . . . dey hab some chillun wut didn't hab duh powwu tuh fly."[1]

What does gravity mean when folks can fly? The stories of slaves who flew away to escape the horrors of plantation life abound, but have particular relevance in the Georgia Sea Islands. The narratives do not make reference to emotional or psychological escapes, but to mythic and spiritual realities that inspired the lives of those bent over cotton plants.

On one level, the stories are narrative constructs designed to restore hope, but, on another level, soaring above oppression is real, and the very best part of the story is that the secret flight was kept from those who believed that they owned dark bodies. Flight was unassailable proof to the contrary.

In her book *The Sea Birds Are Still Alive*, Toni Cade Bambara captured the elegance of the flight stories and the dissonance between Eurocentric and indigenous worldviews. In one of her stories, Fess Newton is in the midst of one of those kitchen-table discussions where knowledge is dispensed and rivals are debated. In lieu of traditional village gatherings, barbershops and kitchen tables in the African American community became centers for the dispensation of knowledge through storytelling.

---

1. Phyllis Green, as cited in *Cut Loose Your Stammering Tongue: Black Theology in the Slave Narratives*, ed. Dwight N. Hopkins and George Cummings (Maryknoll, NY: Orbis, 1991), 70–71. See also Stacy I. Morgan, "Dust Tracks Untrampled by the Dinosaur of History: The Ibo's Landing and Flying Africans Narratives as Mythic Counter-Memory," Graduate Institute of Liberal Arts, Emory University, Atlanta, Georgia; and Janice Liddell, *Imani and the Flying Africans* (New York: Africa World Press, 1994).

It was here that the griots assembled. Fess Newton is one who has forgotten how to soar. He is now an initiate in the school of reason and logic and is attempting the impossible task of explaining why it is scientifically impossible for human beings to fly. It is clear that Bambara wanted us to zero in on the cultural and scientific significance of the dialogue, because she gave Fess Newton a name that evokes both worlds.

Newton starts off reasonably enough with rhetoric about the properties of salt and about positive and negative poles. To support his point, he also offers a convoluted explanation of the laws of gravity. But there is a wiser one present, Ma Hudson, who says,

> "If you can't dance it. . . . And if you can't sing it . . . leastways tell
> it right. Tell it in terms of fire, water, air, earth and bone. It's the
> spirits that—"
> "Same thing," Fess Newton hollering. "Forces is forces. We just
> using different names."[2]

Ma Hudson isn't so easily put off in this battle of words. She proclaims that an explanation, "scientific" or not, isn't worth its salt if you can't dance to it: "Tell it right with the right names for the things, stead of all this electro whatever. Make it sound like a coffeepot perkin. Can't nobody dance to that. My feet ain't even tapping."[3]

But what is she talking about? Could it be the same point that Bernice Johnson Reagon, former historian at the Smithsonian Institute and founder of the singing group Sweet Honey in the Rock, makes in her video "The Songs Are Free"? Reagon says that when she begins to sing, her body gets flushed and every fiber of her being changes. She can feel the song resonating and resurrecting her interiority.[4]

Native American scholar Vine Deloria, Jr. made a similar claim. Writing

---

2. Toni Cade Bambara, *The Sea Birds Are Still Alive* (New York: Random House, 1974), 54.

3. Ibid.

4. Bill Moyers and Gail Pellett, "The Songs Are Free: Bernice Johnson Reagon and African American Music," Public Affairs Television, 1991. See also Bernice Johnson Reagon, "Music in the Civil Rights Movement," Interview by Maria Daniels, WGBH Boston, July 2006, *PBS*, https://www.pbs.org/wgbh/americanexperience/features/eyesontheprize-music-civil-rights-movement/.

of the need to denote native ways of approaching scholarship and other academic pursuits, he urged people from the two-thirds world to include the rhythms of the universe in the search for knowledge: "The living universe, in the tribal setting, has its heartbeat, its means of communication, in the drum. . . . Songs become the means of passing information and powers from one species to another."[5]

Hudson, Deloria, and Johnson Reagon know that dance, song, and story connect the human spirit to unseen realities. Their intuitive and experiential beliefs are now supported by science. Both ancient and new sciences agree that the universe is permeated with movement and energy that vibrates and pulsates. In some Eastern Sanskrit traditions, the cosmic sound is named "Anahata Nada," the "Unstruck Sound."[6]

Writer David Gordon contends that there is a significant difference between sounds that occur because one object or entity strikes another, "vibrating together, creating pulsing waves of air molecules which our ears and brains interpret as *sound*," and sounds that occur without direct contact.[7]

The examples of struck sound are familiar—vocal cords, drums, and so forth. However, the sound to which Eastern mystics refer is deemed by some to be "primal energy" generated by the vibration of tiny particles. This description evokes the string theory of quantum physics. This is a theory that describes the fundamental constituent elements of nature as tiny, vibrating, and looped strings.

In even more unusual findings, scientists and musicians are recording the sounds of resonant DNA frequencies. In these projects, "raw data derived from the light absorption spectra of the four bases (adenine, cytosine, thymine, and guanine) that make up the DNA molecule is converted into sonic frequencies."[8] The frequencies are computerized and translated into synthesized sounds, ready for the composer's creative arrangement.

5. Deloria, *For This Land*, 148.

6. David Gordon, "A-U-M Silence . . . the ancient sound of 'OM,'" http://www.spiritsound.com/aum.html.

7. Ibid.

8. "The Music of DNA: The Building Block of Life," introduction to the recording *Sequencia*, composed by Susan Alexjander in partnership with cell biologist David Deamer (1990).

Dale Pond, a specialist in sympathetic vibratory physics, writes, "Genesis records God as having *said* Light into Being but perhaps it would be more accurate to say God *sang* Light into Being as the prelude to our cosmic dance."[9]

Jesus gives a sly hint that perhaps it is as Pond suggests. After the Last Supper, the God Son steps out into the night with the disciples and heads toward an uncertain fate, but with a song. Mark 14:26 (NRSV) says, "And when they had sung the hymn, they went out to the Mount of Olives." Perhaps the resonance of the song held them in a moment of unity that could be recalled in the troubled days that were just ahead of them. Music, dance, and stories have upheld hopeful people throughout the ages.

As it turns out, flying slaves are no more or less bizarre than DNA hit tunes or the *sotto voce* rumble of elephants engaged in plodding conversations that humans can't hear. Even dancing is amenable to the analysis of physicists and biologists through the discipline of kinesiology (the study of human movement). Why are we surprised? From the Gullah circle dance to the Pentecostal shout and Native American Ghost Dance, every primal culture connected music, song, and dance to spiritual realms and the order of the cosmos.

Our recent awareness of the hum of the earth and the vibrations of our own inner energy speak to the dynamism of a universe that is stranger than we can imagine. In the realm of quantum mechanics, as particles dance in chaotic but harmonious patterns, one wonders how the elders knew that music, dance, and storytelling were intrinsic to an indivisible world of experience, relationships, and science. Science speaks of a universe that vibrates and hums with energy; religion speaks of a God who also weeps and sings. The cultures of the two-thirds world bring these concepts into harmony through ritual and myth.

Choose Your Mythology

MYTHOLOGIES DIFFER FROM culture to culture, vary from time to time. Old mythologies are replaced by new stories; one culture borrows from

---

9. Dale Pond, "It Really Is a Musical Universe!" *Sympathetic Vibratory Physics*, November 1999, https://www.svpvril.com/musicuni.html.

another. According to cultural theorist Jack Solomon, the myths that frame our perspective and beliefs are generally invisible to us as myths so long as they seem to correspond to reality. Once the frame begins to appear, the myth's authority weakens and a new myth takes its place.[10]

The discussion of Africans flying may be considered mythology in scientific circles; however, science has its own mythologies. The words that we choose to describe events provide the lens or framework that directs our gaze. Dominant cultures have directed their collective gaze toward models of study and analysis that rely on rationality, logic, and repeatable experiments. It is only in retrospect that ethnic people have learned that those who control the methodologies and choose the questions can also decide how to use and interpret information.

Jack Solomon argues that scientists don't make observations or conduct experiments for "the sake of knowledge alone." The reasons for a particular emphasis might include personal ambition, altruism, history, or even politics.[11] Scientists work within communities and are influenced by agreed-upon norms and axioms.[12] As is the case in most disciplines, established knowledge is the tether that constrains discovery.

> The invisible college of scientists reaches certain conclusions, less because nature actually takes this particular form, but because the college has unconsciously decided to describe nature in this way.... Nature often resists our prior expectations and the eventual discovery, when it comes, is frequently very surprising, beyond our powers to have anticipated beforehand. (The discovery of quantum theory was an extreme example of this kind.)[13]

10. Jack Solomon, *The Signs of Our Time: The Secret Meanings of Everyday Life* (New York: Harper & Row, 1988), 57. See also David B. Feldman, "The Paradoxical Secret to Finding Meaning in Life: Searching for Meaning Might Backfire," *Psychology Today*, May 18, 2018, https://www.psychologytoday.com/us/blog/supersurvivors/201805/the-paradoxical-secret-finding-meaning-in-life.

11. During the 1930s, some German scientists had the gall to call Einstein's work "Jewish physics." Later, these same scientists would deem their own demonic experiments on a captive Jewish population normative.

12. Polkinghorne, *Science and Theology*, 12.

13. Ibid., 12–13.

It is clear that the emphasis given to particular aspects of reality tends to influence priorities and research funding. It is difficult to support research in fields that are not deemed "serious" or normative. Dominant cultures invest the words "serious" and "value" with a great deal of power to ward off the inference that Western science is just another mythology with its own shamans, sacred language, and ritual.

Yet many Western scientific practices are similar to earlier mythological ones. Whereas ancestors sought the advice of healers and spiritualists, we seek the blessings of scientists on issues ranging from earthquake predictions to lost Mars explorers to tomorrow's weather. To one extent or another, every discourse is a primal human response to an enigmatic cosmos.

Europeans participate in these primal responses because they are also indigenous people with a history of healers and shamans. The varied tribes that inhabited Europe after the fall of Rome left evidence of cultic worship and sacred sites where stone temples were built to reverence the winter solstice and equinox. These historical realities about Euro-tribal origins did not become sources of discomfort until the nineteenth century.

With the advent of the age of reason, both theology and science retreated from mythology and public debate. Both were lulled into the belief that the stories of the elders didn't matter. According to Brian Swimme, "Modern humanity seems to be the first culture to break with this primordial tradition of celebrating the mysteries of the universe. Instead, life has been divided into smaller and smaller categories of engagement."[14]

Yet, even as we retreat, the inferences, whispers, and stories of the griots about multiple realities, connections, and uncertainty as a viable modality are being confirmed. Even though the mathematical languages chosen to transmit this information hinder the access of everyday folks, the principles and philosophies that are emerging are vitally important to expand our closed discussions about race.

---

14. Brian Swimme, *Canticle to the Cosmos* (Louisville, CO: Sounds True, 1995), MP3, 9 hours.

Remembering the Shamans:
Knowledge in Primal and Postmodern Configurations

THERE ARE MANY WAYS to explore and express what it means to be human. Sometimes instinct, memory, and shamans are our guides. "There is a reason, after all, that some people wish to colonize the moon, and others dance before it as before an ancient friend. . . . All [humans] are primitive, but it can be doubted that all [humans] are primitive in the same way."[15]

I have been in the company of shamans. I remember an evening that extended into a night and into the next day. We gathered in a hotel suite to sit at the feet of the legendary author James Baldwin (1924–1987). As the night wore on, he and his brother matched wits with unabashed adoration for one another. They waxed eloquent, regaling us with tall tales and anecdotes. As it is with all shamans, the time passed in a way that is still present with me but belongs to a waking dream state.

I wish that I could remember the details of our conversation, but every cell of my body remembers Baldwin's spirit and our sense of unity. I am very clear about what we didn't talk about. We did not speak of King's assassination. Those of us who had marched and prayed with King still owned the grief in catastrophic ways and worked daily to keep the sorrow from erupting yet again.

Instead, we wondered about the community-called-beloved. It is what Baldwin talked about and didn't. It was what was said and wasn't. For one short evening, hearing the stories of the past and the collective longing for a future, we remembered who we truly are.

Remembering who we are is difficult when every aspect of life in the twenty-first century is organized to make us forget, but such difficulty is not new to our century. In the North American diaspora, Africans were denied the use of native languages, rituals, and associations in the days of missionization and conversion, just as Native American people were urged to forget the ways of their ancestors, and Hispanic and Jewish people were encouraged to change names that identified their ethnicity.

---

15. James Baldwin, *No Name in the Street* (New York: Dial, 1972), 193–194.

The image of the melting pot became the metaphor that erased difference and molded an image of the quintessential "American." Today, culture erodes as a result of neglect. In an era of techno-everything, who has time to sit by the fire with a griot to hear the story of ancestors' feats or tribal origins? Today, many workers have become wandering nomads, following the corporate demands of postmodernity, while delegating elder- and childcare to market forces.[16] Despite this forced mobility across national and state boundaries, and the diversification of the workplace and the nation, Eurocentric views of value and scientific validity still predominate.

Even when specific benefits or goods are gleaned from the people of two-thirds-world nations, the knowledge that accompanies those indigenous products is often rejected or co-opted.[17] In the cultural fields where we sojourn, there are vast stores of human wisdom that can be gathered as a welcome harvest, but dominant cultures are not organized to process values and ideologies that don't match Western norms.

People from two-thirds-world nations are not waiting for political, historical, or even religious shifts of power paradigms. They want to be certain that both science and religion enhance the common good and their ability to survive systemic assaults against their humanity. Toward that end, they are devising methodologies that reflect their own perspectives of the cosmos.

---

16. Lecture and conversations with Ched Myers, New Testament scholar, spring 2000 lecture series, Memphis Theological Seminary, Memphis, Tennessee. See also recent articles by Ched Myers at https://chedmyers.org/.

17. The recent interest in new, plant-based pharmaceuticals provides a good example. Inevitably, exploitative business interests are translating the experiential knowledge of local healers into corporate profits. Those who hoped that the advent of information technology would level the epistemological playing field have found that North American values, ideologies, and worldviews are spreading via the Internet in ways that tend to overpower the small, the indigenous, and the local sites of human endeavor and wisdom.

The Scientific Methodologies of Ethnic People

From an indigenous perspective coming to know is connecting to the universal energy—the source of life.[18]

THE DEVELOPMENT OF indigenous methods of scientific inquiry is both a creative and defensive move. So much has been stolen or appropriated that the language of protest is inadequate to awaken the dominant culture to the devastating consequences of centuries of cultural insensitivity. Why, for example, are the graves of white pilgrims revered and the burial sites of indigenous people dug up and desecrated in the name of science?

At one annual conference of the American Academy of Religion, Native American scholar Vine Deloria, Jr. recited the atrocities of Western scientists and demanded that the bones of the ancestors be returned from museums and archaeological labs. As he spoke, religious scholars filed out of the room in a steady trickle. Some seemed embarrassed and chagrined by Deloria's strident charges—but, more than that, they were angry that his tone was angry.

It was clear that they missed the point. Polite and reserved academic discourses are inappropriate responses to genocide. El Hajj Malik El Shabazz (Malcolm X) was famous for remarking that if a person sticks a knife in your back and then pulls it out a few inches, you can hardly consider this relief. To the contrary, there is still something to holler about. Deloria felt that he had to raise his voice to alert the communities of the two-thirds-world nations that it is time to reclaim the power to determine their own destinies.

Many ethnic communities profess that they will not submit to scientific study unless they have some control over the research questions and the overall objectives. They have historical reasons for their concerns. Indigenous people often complain that research conducted by members

18. Betty Bastien, "Coming to Know: Research Methodology," Native Research and Scholarship Symposium, Orcas Island, Washington, July 21, 1996. See also K. J. E. Straits et al. and the Guiding Principles Workgroup, *Guiding Principles for Engaging in Research with Native American Communities* (Albuquerque, NM: UNM Center for Rural and Community Behavioral Health & Albuquerque Area Southwest Tribal Epidemiology Center, 2012), https://hsc.unm.edu/vision2020/common/docs/Guiding_Principles_Research_Native_Communities2012.pdf.

of the majority culture is "inaccurate, biased and not told from the tribal perspective."[19]

Scholars can learn only what is spoken, observed, experienced, or written. This would be an acceptable limitation in cultures of the written word. However, many ethnic cultures maintain the bulk of their social understandings and scientific presumptions as an unspoken pool of collective knowledge. Ethnographers who believe that they have captured the essence of an event or ritual may in fact have witnessed a practice that hints at the location of that unspoken and unmapped pool, but such indications barely cause a ripple on the surface of deeply sedimented cultural knowledge.

For some communities, cosmologies are danced, sung, and worn; religion is carved, smoked, and dreamed. For other cultures, laboratories and cathedrals reflect their innate curiosity about the world. Neither is intrinsically more valid than the other. When people generalize about limited and occasional cultural observations, they are usually fundamentally inaccurate. For, even when the collected data is correct, the interpreted conclusion may be incorrect.

As an example, I return to the story of my evening with James Baldwin. If you had been an observer on that night when Baldwin shared a bit of himself with us, what would you have seen? Perhaps an aging novelist who was laughing too hard and drinking too much; perhaps a wide-eyed, insecure literary giant drawing energy from the room. In either case, you would not have seen what occurred. This is not to say that the processes of observation and reporting are not valid; it is to say that some events can't be captured unless the observer can experience the moment. Even at those times, there are aspects of experience that may never be grasped.

What is different about the ethnic/cultural approach to scientific research? Scholars from indigenous cultures profess that primal communities approach life as an undivided whole. Theologian Jamake Highwater (1931–2001) made the observation that the focus seems to be on "the whole question of existence and reality."[20] However, the boundaries of

19. Thomas D. Peacock, "Issues in American Indian Research: The Perspective of a Reservation Indian," American Indian Research Symposium, Orcas Island, Washington, July 1996, 4. See also recent reports from the American Indigenous Research Association: http://www.americanindigenousresearchassociation.org/.

20. Jamake Highwater, *The Primal Mind: Vision and Reality in Indian America* (New

that reality are permeable and flexible enough to encompass dream states, intuition, and discernment.

This is not a romantic assumption. Rather, this worldview is encoded in the myths, rituals, and stories of Africana, Hispanic, Asian, and Native American people. By contrast, Western science is marked by the attempt to contain the contours of reality between the limited spaces and synapses of human rationality.

A few years ago, the Native Research and Scholarship Committee met to discuss basic values for indigenous research methodologies.[21] Their conclusions are congruent with similar discussions in Latin America, Asia, and Africa. Moreover, the principles they decided upon incorporate fluid perceptions of reality. These are the values that guide their research methodologies.

1. *The human family is connected to the Spirit.* In this context, "Spirit" can be understood as the energy of the universe. Western science has found that the smallest elements in the universe are not separate atoms or entities, but instead waves and particles of energy that permeate the cosmos. This energy is deemed to be a manifestation of human/divine potential and creative interaction.[22]

   Physicist David Bohm (1917–1992) discussed the implicate order of waves and particles as well as the explicate order or constant motion of energy. He wrote, "The explicate order is that which Indigenous peoples may refer to as the source of life or the spiritual energies of the universe."[23] In fact, "one of the first principles of Indigenous science is that the universe is made up of spiritual energy."[24] Our existence is integrally tied to this energy.

York: Harper & Row, 1981), 56. See also Peter Kingsley, *A Story Waiting to Pierce You: Mongolia, Tibet and the Destiny of the Western World* (Point Reyes Station, CA: The Golden Sufi Center, 2010).

21. Papers presented at the AIHEC President's Retreat, sponsored by the *Tribal College Journal* et al., Orcas Island, Washington, July 21–22, 1996. Also see updated articles in the *Journal* at https://tribalcollegejournal.org/.

22. F. David Peat, *Lighting the Seventh Fire: The Spiritual Ways, Healing, and Science of the Native American* (New York: Citadel, 1994). See also F. David Peat, *Synchronicity: The Marriage of Matter and Psyche* (Pari, Italy: Pari Publishing Sas, 2014).

23. From Bastien, "Coming to Know," 3, summarizing David Bohm's theory.

24. Ibid.

It is through this energy that we participate in the creation of reality.

Finally, all living entities emit energy. Energy is synonymous with motion and interaction with other volatile and moving life forms. As a consequence, there can be no truly objective observation from a neutral site. Energy skews and affects our efforts to "know" and allows us to participate in the scientific modality while we attempt to observe it.

2. *Reality is relational.* We are all connected through the veil of multiple realities. Neither death nor life can separate us from this intrinsic aspect of the life space. Accordingly, ancestors can advise, and animals and plants can co-labor in the creation process. When this perspective is incorporated into research methodologies, quantitative and qualitative analyses are no longer paramount. Biology can't be separated from law, and physics can't be separated from poetry. Everything is linked through "an indivisible whole . . . and this indivisible whole which we refer to as the universe is affected by the relationship of humanity."[25]

3. *Human beings are "partners with the source of life."*[26] The committee affirmed a belief in the "intelligence" of the universe and our connections through consciousness with a cosmic energy/Spirit. Few can view the order and beauty of the universe without acknowledging its symmetry and balance. Although many scientists adhere to the theory of accidental processes, others see design.

Partnering engenders responsibility, care, and creativity. Hebrew Scripture scholar Terence Fretheim evokes this idea of partnership in his discussion of creation. According to Fretheim's interpretation of the biblical text, God does not create alone, but asks the earth to participate. "Let earth bring forth the living creature according to its kind: cattle and creeping thing and beast of the earth, each according to its kind; and it was so."[27] The earth,

---

25. Ibid., 4.
26. Ibid., 3.
27. Genesis 1:27; Terence Fretheim, Todd Lectures, Memphis Theological Seminary,

as a co-creator, "brings forth"; so do we. In terms of indigenous methodology, creative partnering provides the underlying foundation of any scientific inquiry.

4. *Research goals are subject to community oversight.* Current research offers an alternative to the quantitative analysis that predominates in Western science. Both scientists and community members argue for participatory research, democratic approaches to investigation, and collective analysis of the findings.[28] Participatory research initiatives presume that science is an integral part of the life journey. The questions posed, the methods used to probe for answers, and the interpretation of what is found should be relevant and integral to community.

The community participates in the identification of issues relevant to its interests. "People may participate at different levels depending on the nature of the problem; however, control of the research must always rest with them."[29] This model has pedagogical and political implications for communities that have been routinely divested of power. Ethnic approaches to research modalities incorporate malleable perspectives on "reality" and the use and acknowledgment of permeable borders of space-time.

Indigenous Cosmologies

THERE IS MUCH to be learned from the synthesis of religion, culture, and science in indigenous communities. As Brian Swimme says,

The sciences will just separate the human off and focus on the physical aspects of the universe and the religious traditions will shy away

Memphis, Tennessee, spring 2001. See also Ervin Laszlo and Jude Currivan, *CosMos: A Co-Creator's Guide to the Whole-World* (Carlsbad, CA: Hay House, 2008).

28. Valarie Blue Bird Jernigan, "Community-Based Participatory Research with Native American Communities: The Chronic Disease Self-Management Program," *Health Promotion Practice* 11, no. 6 (November 2010): 888–899.

29. Ibid. See also R. Tandon, "Participatory Research in the Empowerment of People," *Convergence* 14, no. 3 (1981): 20–29.

from the universe because that's reserved for science. So cosmology is an attempt to deal with the whole and the nature of the human in that.[30]

In the earliest days, it was believed that a flat earth and a very present creator capped the creation with a dome that divided waters in a layered firmament. There were no static scientific truths that could be deduced from a firmament that was dependent on the will of God.[31] The flood was proof of that presumption.

Human perception of the natural order confirmed God's constant involvement. Waters parted, plagues fell, the sun stood still. The idea of a flat earth offered a stage for the activities of a hands-on God and a cast of lesser divinities. In most instances, the personalities of the gods mimicked human foibles and triumphs.

Other cosmologies were developing at the same time in cultures around the world. Some ancient people envisioned the cosmos "as a 'cosmic egg,' sometimes as a bowl carried on the back of a turtle."[32] In Egypt, the cosmological surround was formed by the arched body of the goddess Nut, who leaned over the earth god Geb.[33]

Aristotle and Ptolemy honed an earth-centered understanding of the universe that became the dominant perspective of the three monotheistic religions, yet the planets retained the names of the ancient gods.[34] The ability to hold incongruous concepts about reality was a prototype of the uneasy harmony of myth, folly, informed supposition, and observation that engendered shared ideas about the universe.

30. Brian Swimme, "The Universe Story as Sacred Story," in *Fugitive Faith: Interviews by Benjamin Webb* (Maryknoll, NY: Orbis, 1998), 133. See also Brian Swimme, "The Resurgence of Cosmic Storytellers," *The NAMTA Journal* 38, no. 1 (Winter 2013), 165–171, https://files.eric.ed.gov/fulltext/EJ1077950.pdf.

31. Nancy Ellen Abrams and Joel R. Primack, "Cosmology and 21st-Century Culture," *Science* 293, no. 5536 (September 7, 2001): 1769–1770, https://science.sciencemag.org/content/293/5536/1769.full.

32. R. Hanbury Brown, *The Wisdom of Science: Its Relevance to Culture and Religion* (Cambridge, England: Cambridge University Press, 1986), 42. See also Bob Berman, *Strange Universe: The Weird and Wild Science of Everyday Life—On Earth and Beyond* (New York: Times Books, 2003).

33. Ibid.

34. Ibid., 3.

Indigenous societies include science and theology and all other aspects of their culture as a part of their ordinary discourse, for the sciences have never been alienated from daily life. Ancient cosmologies assure us that reality is relational and will not be discovered through a microscope or an intricate mathematical formula; instead, it may be encoded in each event of creation.

The attempt to separate culture and scientific knowledge began during the Enlightenment. Thousands of years earlier, ancient people considered the earth and the cosmos as a living continuum that sustained and permeated them. They did not separate a belief in the spirits and gods from the change of seasons or the struggle to survive. However, the story was primarily religious.

To talk about the scientific methodologies of ethnic people is to talk about origins. From the beginning, the ancestors knew intuitively that knowledge can be life-giving, for without it the people perish. By contrast, one of the legacies of the Enlightenment is that knowledge comes in particular forms and from particular cultures; all else is myth and mystery.

From time immemorial, musings about the origins of the universe permeated the waking and dream worlds of the old and the young. The shift was gradual, from the memories of the griots to the scientific method.

People moved from campfire stories to the mathematical formulas and philosophical deductions of elite scientists and philosophers. Such retreats from the nightly gatherings under the stars inevitably excluded shamans, women, and indigenous folk from the inner circle. Swimme realizes that such exclusions and retreats clouded the collective and individual vision of community members.

> Even though science's violent rejection of every cultural and tribal tradition has been deleterious in the extreme, and even though one can appreciate the vehemence with which fundamentalist religions around the planet reject any compromise with modern secular culture, the opportunity of our time is to integrate science's understanding of the universe with more ancient intuitions concerning the meaning and destiny of the human.[35]

35. Brian Swimme, *The Hidden Heart of the Cosmos: Humanity and the New Story* (Maryknoll, NY: Orbis, 1996), 3.

Swimme urges us to integrate intuitive knowledge, experience, and scientific discoveries. Ancient intuitions hint at expansiveness rather than exclusion, connectedness rather than isolation. The social world that we have created hums an oppositional tune, a murmur of linear progressions, concrete realities, and the ability to develop a theory of everything. Indigenous people peer through experiences and stories, songs and dance, at a world that solicits our attention.

Dancing with Reality

Most people believe that physicists are explaining the world.... They are only dancing with it.

—Gary Zukav, *The Dancing Wu Li Masters*

BUT SCIENTISTS ARE NOT the only people seeking to explain the world, to understand reality. Alfred Schütz (1899–1959) discussed at length the circumstances that lead to a declaration that things are "real."

> Our primitive impulse is to affirm immediately the reality of all that is conceived, as long as it remains uncontradicted. But there are several, probably an infinite number of various orders of realities, each with its own special and separate style of existence.[36]

From our own experiences, we know that reality is not a seamless whole. Multiple realities rise, recede, and eclipse on our cognitive horizons as sub-universes that we inhabit from time to time.[37] These worlds are available to us and are characterized "by peculiar modifications of the basic categories of thought, namely space, time, and causality."[38] The portals to these universes are not always cognitive. Perhaps they can be entered through dance and song and story.

36. Alfred Schütz, "On Multiple Realities," in *Collected Papers 1: The Problem of Social Reality,* ed. Maurice Natanson (The Hague: Martinus Nijhoff, 1962), 207.

37. Alfred Schütz, "Don Quixote and the Problem of Reality," in *Collected Papers 2: Studies in Social Theory,* ed. Arvid Brodersen (The Hague: Martinus Nijhoff, 1964), 135–158.

38. Ibid., 139.

The superstring theory provides useful analogies for indigenous studies. Physicist Brian Greene writes, "If string theory is right, the microscopic fabric of our universe is a richly intertwined multidimensional labyrinth within which the strings of the universe endlessly twist and vibrate, rhythmically beating out the laws of the cosmos."[39] The theory speaks of universes coiled into infinitesimal loops that may hold the secrets of all forces in the cosmos. The beauty of the theory is that it is dynamic and rhythmic. It is a resonant and dancing universe that invites us to view its mysteries.

Engaging the Cosmos:
The Thing Unnamed

FOR INDIGENOUS PEOPLE, the stories hint of something unspoken. Theologian Megan McKenna and storyteller Tony Cowan refer to this element as "the thing not named."

> In more theological or religious terms it is the Midrash, the underlying truth, the inspired layers that are hinted at, that invite but do not force themselves upon us. They must be searched out, struggled with and taken to heart. It is, at root, the mystery that makes the story memorable, worth telling over and over again, and staking your life on.[40]

Hopi elders engage multiplicity by referring to the ineffable as "a mighty something." Wisdom instructs the elders that one cannot stake life on limited human perspectives. There must be more, and so the elders inquire into the nature of ontology, social location, and the universe with the humble acceptance of an abiding wonder for "the thing not named."

Theologian Theophus Smith discusses the engagement of African

39. Brian Greene, *The Elegant Universe: Superstrings, Hidden Dimensions, and the Quest for the Ultimate Theory* (New York: Vintage, 1999), 18. For updates on string theory, listen to Sean Carroll's podcast *Mindscape*, episode 31, "Brian Greene on the Multiverse, Inflation, and the String Theory Landscape," January 28, 2019.

40. Megan McKenna and Tony Cowan, *Keepers of the Story* (Maryknoll, NY: Orbis, 1997), 66.

American communities with "the mighty something . . . the thing not named" as symbolic and ritual transformations of the life space that may be unorthodox, but are neither irrational nor evidence of the occult.

[Conjure is] more than a mere metaphor, it is a magical means of transforming reality, a way in which humanity maps and manages the world. As a primordial, yet enduring, system of communication in all cultures, it is in fact, a form of language. A language which employs ritual speech.[41]

Some Eurocentric perspectives connect conjure with witchcraft and sorcery, while Afrocentric uses and understandings of conjure usually elicit communal practices and beliefs that helped to resist white supremacy.[42] New Testament scholar Clarice Martin uses a similar analysis of the conjure or hoodoo practices of Marie Laveau (1801–1881) and others. She says that hoodoo "ameliorated dysfunction and disharmony in the community. It was retributive and supportive."[43]

The origin of the term "hoodoo" is unknown. Some connect the word to voodoo, vodou, or vodun, but there are differences. Vodou refers to the communal and religious mediation of energy, spirit, and nature through West African cultural practices. Hoodoo blends the cosmology and practices of Yoruban, Ifa, European perspectives, Jewish mysticism, and American Indian herbal knowledge.[44] This is a syncretistic expression of cultural and religious practices. In such systems, reality does not obey the rules of a sequential and orderly world. Instead, the life space offers a multiplicity of options in a multiverse, where hoodoo, vodun, and a variety of faith systems can coexist.

---

41. Theophus H. Smith, as quoted in Martin, "Hoodoo Man," 4, 5.

42. Theophus H. Smith, *Conjuring Culture: Biblical Formations of Black America* (New York: Oxford University Press, 1994), 4.

43. Martin, "Hoodoo Man," 205.

44. Patti Wigington, "Hoodoo—What is Hoodoo?" *Learn Religions*, July 5, 2019, https://www.learnreligions.com/what-is-hoodoo-2561899.

Africana Culture and the Cosmos

INTEREST IN THE historical retrieval of sub-Saharan African archaeo-astronomy is relatively recent, but there is evidence of scientific engagement on the African continent that may rival European probes of the cosmos. Whether this information can be recovered is not known at this time, but initial findings are intriguing.

Among the Borana, a Nilotic people of southern Ethiopia and northwest Kenya, researchers B. M. Lynch and L. H. Robbins observed stone megaliths in 1978 that seemed to have spiritual and cosmological origins. The site is at mystical Lake Turkana. The mirages on the lake make spatial references difficult; the fish drawn from the lake are large and unusual to the Western eye.

The local people refer to the stones in their community as "Namora-tunga," meaning stone people.[45] When I visited the area, I felt as though I had entered another space-time dimension. Archaeologists are not exactly sure of the meaning of the stones, which are magnetic, but they think that the Borana calendar used "six star positions marked by seven stars or star groups."[46] Computer analyses of the alignments indicate a congruence with star positions in 300 BCE.

There are other connections between Africa and the cosmos. The kingdom of Kush in central Sudan (1000 BCE–200 CE) has pyramids that may be aligned with the star Sirius in a manner reminiscent of Egyptian cosmologies and pyramid formations. In Zimbabwe, archaeological ruins of the Shona people seem to mark astronomical events of their time.

Finally, there is the controversial story of the Dogon and the star Sirius B. Sirius A is, according to astronomers, the brightest star in the sky and played an important role in Egyptian cosmology. However, it was not

---

45. B. M. Lynch and L. H. Robbins, "Namoratunga: The First Archeoastronomical Evidence in Sub-Saharan Africa," *Science* 200, no. 4343 (June 1978): 766–768.

46. Laurence R. Doyle and Edward W. Frank, "Astronomy in Africa," *Encyclopaedia of the History of Science, Technology, and Medicine in Non-Western Cultures*, ed. Helaine Selin (Norwell, MA: Kluwer Academic Publishers, 1997), 96. Some archaeologists believe that the stones mark burial sites. See also L. R. Doyle and T. J. Wilcox, "Statistical Analysis of Namoratunga: An Archaeoastronomical Site in Sub-Saharan Africa?" *Azania: Journal of the British Institute of East Africa* 21 (1986): 125–129 and Christine Mullen Kreamer, *African Cosmos* (New York: Monacelli, 2012).

until 1844 that Friedrich Bessel (1784–1846) deduced from a slight wobble (which can indicate gravitational pull) that Sirius A might have a twin star that was hidden from view. Named Sirius B, this smaller but denser star was not seen until 1862, when Alvan Graham Clark (1832–1897) viewed it through the strongest telescope available at the time.[47]

Sirius B is a white dwarf, meaning that it is a star like our sun. It is one of the densest forms of matter, other than neutron stars. When anthropologist Marcel Griaule (1898–1956) researched the folklore of the Dogon, he found evidence that they knew of the dwarf star before it was seen through the telescope. In fact, they knew that Po Tolo (the Dogon name for Sirius B) was heavy, white, and circled Sirius A every fifty years. Their ceremonies every fifty years to celebrate the completion of the cycle were documented by ceremonial masks that date back to the thirteenth century.[48] The Dogon also predicted the existence of a third satellite star around Sirius that has not yet been seen, but the possibility of its existence has not been ruled out. The Dogon stories include knowledge that can be verified and knowledge that abides in the thin spaces of dream dimensions.

Because the Dogon were a relatively isolated African culture, Western scientists have been reluctant to attribute this knowledge to advanced observational skills or scientific acumen. Many theories exist to explain or dismiss the phenomenon, including the supposition that Anglo adventurers, missionaries, and scientists may have shared information about ancient astronomical projections about the existence of Sirius B.

Those who ascribe to this theory cannot explain why rock drawings of tribal cosmological knowledge predate contact with Europeans. The Dogon have told us a different story, of ancient space visitors named the Nommos, who shared their knowledge of the cosmos, arrived by airship, and left in the same way with a promise to return.

The narratives that have evolved around Dogon cosmology are mystical and ceremonial; however, there is a practical component to their belief system. The Dogon connected the cycles of Sirius B with fonio grain, which is small, white, and heavy like the hidden star. The Egyptians connected Sirius A with the flooding of the Nile. It may be impossible to

47. Doyle and Frank, "Astronomy in Africa," 99.
48. Ibid., 100.

prove, one way or another, the source of their knowledge, but the story should be told. The children of the African diaspora should know that their ancestors also looked up and considered the cosmos as an integral part of their lives.[49]

In North America, cosmology played an important part in slave escapes to freedom. They knew that freedom was north and they knew that the North Star (Polaris) could guide their feet. The North Star is located at the end of the Little Dipper. As slaves used hollowed-out gourds to dip water, they renamed the constellation "the drinking gourd" to match their own cultural understanding.[50]

However, many natural obstacles stood between the star and the land journey. After a few mishaps, members of the Underground Railroad began to send teachers south to teach the slaves the most advantageous route.

The routes were sometimes taught in coded map songs. One particular song is entitled "Follow the Drinking Gourd." An old man named Peg Leg Joe is said to have passed the information from plantation to plantation. Some say that Joe is a composite character while others insist that he was an actual person. The song taught slaves to leave during winter so that they would encounter a frozen Ohio River that would be easier to traverse. The words are poignant:

> When the sun comes back and the
> first quail calls follow the drinking gourd.
> For the old man is a-waiting
> for to carry you to freedom,
> if you follow the drinking gourd.
> The river bank will make a very good road,
> the dead trees will show you the way,
> left foot, peg foot, traveling on,
> follow the drinking gourd.

49. For further information about the Dogon, see Marcel Griaule, *Conversations with Ogotemmêli: An Introduction to Dogon Religious Ideas* (London: Oxford University Press, 1965), 97–200. See also Laird Scranton, *The Science of the Dogon: Decoding the African Mystery Tradition* (Rochester, VT: Inner Traditions, 2006).

50. The direction of escape depended on location. Not all slaves went north. Some headed for Native American communities, Mexico, or islands in the Caribbean.

RACE AND THE COSMOS

The river ends between two hills.
Follow the drinking gourd.
There's another river on the other side,
follow the drinking gourd.

Where the great big river meets
the little river, follow the drinking gourd.
For the old man is a-waiting to carry
you to freedom if you follow
the drinking gourd.[51]

Once again music, movement, and rhetoric/teaching are the components that liberate. The environmental signposts guide seekers of freedom; the songs connect to the basic elements of spirit and matter.

African Cultural Examples and Scientific Theory

ENGAGING THE THING unnamed becomes a very specific practice in the two examples that I offer for consideration. First, Reginald Crosley initiates a unique discussion of reality in relation to vodou in his book *The Vodou Quantum Leap: Alternate Realities, Power, and Mysticism*. In it, he finds connections between hyperspace and the trance states that are integral to vodou practices.

Vodou is an African religion that has its roots in Dahomey, present-day Nigeria, Benin, and Togo. "Vodou" is a Fon word for God/Spirit, which can take many forms. During slavery, Vodou was adapted to the diasporan context in the Americas, with a particular concentration in Haiti. Ceremonies include dimensional interaction between spirits and community members. I am reminded of the theory of hyperspace, which suggests there are more than the four space-time dimensions that we are able to perceive. In fact, physicists contend that there may be many universes, suspended and separate, except for the possibility of wormhole tunnels that may connect them and allow travel between the worlds.[52]

---

51. "Educator's Guide to *Follow the Drinking Gourd*," New Jersey State Museum Planetarium and Raritan Valley Community College Planetarium.
52. Michio Kaku, *Hyperspace: A Scientific Odyssey Through Parallel Universes, Time*

Crosley submits the possibility that communication between universes may be "non-local." Like healing prayers that don't require direct contact to be efficacious, the vehicle of communication in vodou may be the trance state. During ritual trance states, initiates solicit spirits called *loa* (ancestral spirits) from other realms, which inhabit the seeker's body.

There are several good historical films that show the depth of trance and the ease with which the seeker and the spirits move from one reality to another. Crosley notes that the fact that vodou is an immaterial force does not mean that it is not "real" or physical. In quantum physics, wave and particle functions seem to be immaterial but are still part of the physical world.[53]

The discussion of the material and immaterial takes us to the heart of Crosley's argument. According to Crosley, "Our body is composed of packets, bundles, or quanta of energy, giving us a localization, a position in space-time; while at the same time, the wave-function aspect is all over the cosmos continuum."[54] Crosley views the vodou world as parallel to our everyday objective world and in affinity with the theory of hyperspace. Similar arguments could be made from other faith perspectives. Although the human community is confined to four dimensions, string theory offers a ten-dimensional universe with ample opportunities to situate the unexplained within its folds.[55]

The second example comes from Dagara scholar Malidoma Patrice Somé's study *Of Water and the Spirit: Ritual, Magic, and Initiation in the Life of an African Shaman*. Somé describes the initiation and his grandfather's death as events that suspend the ordinary laws of nature.

Warps, and the 10th Dimension (New York: Anchor, 1995), 3–29. See also Michio Kaku, *Physics of the Future: How Science Will Shape Human Destiny and Our Daily Lives by the Year 2100* (New York: Doubleday, 2011).

53. Reginald Crosley, *The Vodou Quantum Leap: Alternate Realities, Power, and Mysticism* (St. Paul, MN: Llewellyn, 2000), 86; see also footnote 1. A revised and expanded edition is now available (München, Germany: Theion Publishing, 2014).

54. Ibid., 48. From this perspective, Jesus' attestation, "Lo, I am with you always" (Matthew 28:20) takes on a very pragmatic nuance. If human beings can be here, there, and everywhere despite the appearance of a fixed spatial position, then we need to attend seriously to our relationships.

55. In bosonic string theory, spacetime is 26-dimensional, while in superstring theory it is 10-dimensional and in M-theory it is 11-dimensional.

The most telling examples of the altered reality structure include pots that cook upside down on the ceiling, defying gravity. Grandfather dies in the missionary hospital and, after death, he is walked home using a ritual object. The purported powers of this object contradict the scientific laws of this realm.

Grandfather walks slowly, of course, but, as Somé notes, the dead aren't in a hurry. Somé offers an explanation for this event that gives one pause: "Why do the dead walk where I come from? They walk because they are still as important to the living as they were before."[56] Prior to his death, Grandfather prepares Somé by saying, "Know only that where I exist is not on the earth, but in a universe of its own. I see you better from there than I ever could from here."[57] Clearly, Grandfather's power does not abate with his death.

Indigenous cultures often invest power in unlikely members of society. It is the elderly, shamans, misfits, and maidens who are given the power to initiate the young, mediate disputes, and intercede in other realms. Those who saw visions and talked to themselves were the bearers of culture.

Somé tells of his adult initiation into the rituals of an African culture that struggled to retain its integrity during the assault of missionization. He reports that the elders wore clothing that symbolized the accumulation of knowledge and power. The clothing was ragged, smelly, and tattered, not because the elders were ignorant of personal hygiene, but because power had nothing to do with aesthetics or material goods. Power is seen as a spiritual force that sustains the community and guides individuals. Somé says, "As long as we are not ourselves, we will try to be what other people are. If these people are also not themselves, the result is terrible."[58] It was the elders' connection to other realities that enhanced wisdom, self-respect, and continuity in the community.

56. Malidoma Patrice Somé, *Of Water and the Spirit: Ritual, Magic, and Initiation in the Life of an African Shaman* (New York: Penguin, 1994), 47.
57. Ibid., 27.
58. Ibid., 288.

Summary

IF, AS HAVEL and Bambara propose, transcendence is the only real alternative to extinction, then the human task becomes more fascinating and difficult than one can conceive. First, we must remember who we were before we inhabited geo-cultural locations that emphasize sameness. In North America, the delusion of sameness is a web cast from shore to shore in ways that make ethnic diversity even more startling than one would suppose.

If the United States is now organized so that most cities not only look alike in a Disneyesque parody, and all food over thousands of miles is packaged and marketed to taste the same, how can we be expected to stomach difference? Palates programmed to ingest bland familiarities will vomit the stranger from the craw.

Yet Westerners are not as alienated from indigenous perspective as it would seem. Every culture, no matter where it currently stands, emerged from basic and primal human organizations. It is in the remembrance that we reconnect to our relationship to the universe. Maybe if we can remember, we'll be able to fly.

As Granddaddy Sanders says in Bambara's short story, "Broken Field Running," "I was saying that we could fly, but we got messed around with all that salt. Salt treks, salt trails, all those mother's tears, all those bones bleaching in the briny deep, all that sweat."[59] To be certain, salt is the historical reality for many in the two-thirds world, but soaring is the future.

We are finding through our telescopes and mathematical formulations that life is neither linear nor progressive, and it certainly isn't hierarchical. It is chaotic, unpredictable, and stunning in its creative complexities. "Objectivity" in its modernist form is a fallen house of cards. Accordingly, we can no longer give special credence to a dominant theory or story about why things are the way that they appear to be unless we include the equally valid suppositions of other cultures.

59. Bambara, *The Sea Birds*, 54.

five

⠿

Understanding something you cannot see
is difficult—but not impossible.
Not surprisingly, astronomers currently study dark matter
by its effects on the bright matter that we do observe. . . .
When we watch a nearby star wobbling predictably,
we infer from calculations that a "dark planet"
orbits around it.

—Vera Rubin,
"Dark Matter in the Universe"

⠿

Sometimes we are blessed
with being able to choose the time,
and the arena, and the manner of our revolution,
but more usually we must do battle
where we are standing.

—Audre Lorde,
Sister Outsider: Essays and Speeches

⠿

⁙ 5 ⁙

Race, Cosmology, and Belonging

Racism is a punk.
It is so fragile.
It is so easily suspended.
Anything I can suspend isn't real.
—Dick Gregory

As you keep pulling back the layers of how deeply rooted anti-blackness and white supremacy are in this country, it is exhausting and it is traumatizing.

—Alicia Garza

If eyes can be trained to see darkness as a contributing symbol, perhaps other needed reorientations can happen as well.

—Larry Rasmussen,
Earth Community, Earth Ethics

D ICK GREGORY (1932–2017) exposes racism's complex nature with his satirical jab. Anyone who has been on the receiving end of racism's clenched fist knows that it is very real, extremely resilient, and, as Garza notes, very traumatizing. But Gregory is correct to point out the fleeting, cowardly, and elusive quality of oppression. It can be hidden, suppressed, and suspended. Even when it stands before the whole world, in all of its vile configurations, its existence can be denied. Yet, there is something unnerving about Gregory's assertion. We know from experience and history that racialized rhetoric has a permanency that defies efforts at deconstruction.[1] Racism may be a punk, but it is also a principality with structural manifestations that persist for generations.

The conundrum of racism's permanence and elusiveness in North American contexts reminds me of the children's story, "The Emperor's New Clothes."[2] In this fable, adults ignore the king's nudity in public places, pretending that all is well. It takes a child to point out that the emperor is not wearing clothes. Racism, however, is not so easily revealed.

If you point to racism like the child pointed to the emperor, yelling for all you are worth that it is naked and in our midst, those who deny its existence will not address the emperor's state of undress. They will simply say that there is no emperor. The problem in the fable can be remedied by encouraging observers to report what they actually see.

But as we approach the year 2020, some argue that we should abandon or add modifiers to the word "racism" because, alone, it is too general to describe what is actually happening to people of color. Instead, they suggest that we add words like "anti-black"[3] or "anti-immigrant" to describe

---

1. Discussions with Victor Anderson during the Lived Theology Project, Oxford, Mississippi, February 2001.

2. Hans Christian Andersen, "The Emperor's New Clothes," trans. Jean Hersholt (New York: Limited Editions Club, 1949).

3. The Movement for Black Lives provides the following definitions on their website (https://policy.m4bl.org/glossary):

"Anti-Black: The Council for Democratizing Education defines anti-Blackness as being a two-part formation that both voids Blackness of value, while systematically marginalizing Black people and their issues. The first form of anti-Blackness is overt racism. Society also associates [politically incorrect] comments with the overt nature of anti-Black racism. Beneath this anti-Black racism is the covert structural and systemic racism which categorically predetermines the socioeconomic status of Blacks in this country.

the lethal specificity of oppression. I agree that clarity is important when we are describing oppression, but I also believe that the word "racism" is still useful and descriptive.

Racism is an equal-opportunity oppression that is not easily resolved. Poet Audre Lorde wrote this about the problem:

> Eventually institutional racism becomes a question of power and privilege rather than merely color, which then serves as a subterfuge. The connections between Africans and African-Americans, African-Europeans, African-Asians, is real . . . and we all need to examine without sentimentality or stereotype what the injection of Africanness into the socio-political consciousness of the world could mean. We need to join our differences and articulate our particular strengths in the service of our mutual survivals, and against the desperate backlash which attempts to keep that Africanness from altering the very bases of current world power and privilege.[4]

Lorde wrote of the devastation that racism and sexism leave in their wake, while philosopher Jacques Derrida (1930–2004) wrote of the unexpected consequences of oppression. Derrida reminded us that naming isn't the solution to all of our social problems. In fact, he wrote, "Monsters cannot be announced. One cannot say: 'here are our monsters,' without immediately turning the monsters into pets."[5]

In a very enigmatic way, racism has become such a pet. We have marched, discussed, and debated until the snarling, dangerous monster

---

The structure is held in place by anti-Black policies, institutions, and ideologies.

"The second form of anti-Blackness is the unethical disregard for anti-Black institutions and policies. This disregard is the product of class, race, and/or gender privilege certain individuals experience due to anti-Black institutions and policies. This form of anti-Blackness is protected by the first form of overt racism.

"Anti-Black Racism: Term used to specifically describe the unique discrimination, violence and harms imposed on and impacting Black people specifically."

4. Audre Lorde, *A Burst of Light: Essays by Audre Lorde* (Ithaca, NY: Firebrand, 1988), 37–38.

5. Jacques Derrida, "Some Statements and Truisms about Neologisms, Newisms, Postisms, Parasitisms, and other Small Seismisms," in *The States of "Theory": History, Art, and Critical Discourse*, ed. David Carroll (New York: Columbia University Press, 1989), 80.

seems strangely domesticated and familiar. In North American communities and throughout the world, racism is infused into every aspect of life. Those who are deemed to be victims live within the paradox of resistance, assimilation, and appropriation.

Whenever the need arises, victims parade the monster before society as an object of museum-quality fear. They are immune to its bite, having lived with the compromises and daily enticements to coexist with and become what they hate. For oppressors, the monster's domestication is proof that the danger no longer exists. The language of protest is familiar, the monster has been announced, and we seem to be stuck with a very dangerous pet.

An Invitation to View the World Differently

THE DISCOURSES OF DIFFERENCE have focused on the struggle for acceptance, equal social options, and established rights, but the study of cosmology teaches us that the desire for belonging that lures those on the margins to seek its embrace doesn't exist as a stable or tangible target. Rather, issues of equality and acceptance are also matters of the spirit that can't be mandated or imposed. We have tried the juridical option with only the most superficial gains to show for our efforts. Even though we have labeled those gains "success," in retrospect they seem so slight and so superfluous that a sense of failure pervades even the greatest of triumphs.

Well-meaning people wonder where the cause for racial equality was derailed. Why did Watts erupt five days after the signing of the Voting Rights Act, with a death toll of thirty-five? I often wonder whether the strategic focus on particular social issues shifted our collective purposes. While historic battles for equality had to focus on particularities—that is, the integration of schools, lunch counters, and workplaces—the philosophical skirmish has to be about much more.

Struggles for liberation are attempts to shift realities, to invite the community to see the world differently. This purpose is muted and eventually lost when people are snared on oppression's grinding wheel. When you use your power and perceptions of difference to kill me, I must do something. If I am a slave, I may steal your pig, grind glass into your grits, or run for freedom. Whether I am a woman, LGBTQIA+, or a child laborer in Indonesia, I will resist your determinations that I am not worthy of the goods, blessings, and bounty due to the rest of humankind. In fact, my body, my life, every aspect of my being will refocus on struggle. It will become my discourse, my matrix, my theology.

Those subjected to social abuse respond in any number of ways; the most prevalent responses include fight, flight, or resignation. Those who have engaged in protracted fights for survival often find that the ghost trails of long-forgotten adrenaline surges have carved deep crevasses on the soul.

These scars manifest as the perpetual need to struggle and resist, even when the opposition ends. This is a debilitating life plan that cannot be sustained. Those who flee or resign themselves to the situation often find solace in a discourse of conflict that becomes the only comfortable modality of communication. One wonders if there is any tenable resolution to human angst and conflict. How shall we reveal to one another the things we hold in common? How shall we speak of cosmic connections that are our beginning and ending?

The State of the Union

WE HAVE REACHED a problematic state of being. In the face of worldwide activism, the dominators stopped dominating in the usual ways. They announced détente, *nolo contendere*, no contest. Without admitting guilt, dominators have globally restructured or dispersed systems of oppression and now pretend not to see the support systems that are still in place to maintain control.

Even more confusing is the fact that former victims don't look like victims anymore. Many have access to all the consumer goods that they could possibly want. Moreover, some hold actual and ceremonial positions of power in the political system. So much has changed, and yet everything feels the same.

New connections to universal and cosmic realities are needed to divest malignant systems and their manipulators of historical and narrative advantages and to offer victims alternatives to entrenched and internalized narratives of violation. New questions arise when the language of cosmology is infused into the public dialogue. What does race mean when darkness becomes a metaphor of power and cosmic predominance? Who's in and who's out when connections between cosmological entities can be maintained despite distances of millions of miles? What does individual and communal responsibility mean when potential and limitations are not described as social constructions, but as quantum and cosmic legacies? Despite all of the rhetoric and resistance, the path toward moral flourishing remains obscured by intransigent problems.

Endearing Every Human Face

FROM WHERE DO our ideas about difference come? How are we able to hold on to evil fables about diversity in the face of overwhelming evidence to the contrary? It seems that, early in life, we absorb ethnic mythologies and cultural habituations that affect our thought systems, vocabulary, and reality structures. But these impressions are so subtle that only subliminal footprints are left on the human consciousness. Perhaps that is why it is difficult to trace the origins of our anger and discomforts.

We have learned to like the people and things most like us. The ethereal quality of our discomforts doesn't reveal their rigid and gatekeeping effects. Too often, we allow stereotypes to separate us from one another. By doing so, we limit the horizons of our own creativity and self-awareness. Although people of color are no longer deemed to be "like" children or animals in public rhetoric, they are rendered invisible by the phrase, "I just don't see color." This statement, which usually comes from well-meaning but confused allies, only adds to the mystification of race.

The most pervasive delusion of the last two centuries is that North Americans are color-blind. Cultural critic Michael Eric Dyson points out the difference between Martin Luther King, Jr.'s vision of a colorless society and our own skewed misreading of the idea. He reminds us that King did propose a color-blind society, but only after racism and oppression were destroyed.[6] It is lethal to pretend not to notice color while racism and discrimination still reign, because such attestations silence those who protest against oppression.

During the Civil Rights movement, so many died, so few overcame that efforts toward closure or fulfillment seem premature. Yet the word "premature" seems ill-suited to the context, as the liberationists have been pregnant with hope for more than fifty-five years. One thing is certain: Striving and overcoming, resisting and rebelling are not the same as giving birth. There have been some gains, but catastrophic losses even the tally, and still we hold out the hope of a better and more egalitarian society. Perhaps our hope persists because the phrase "We shall overcome" is such an affirmative, rhetorical statement about the justice of God's order and the dedication of those seeking relief that we just insist that it has to come true.

In the event that it doesn't, narrative and rhetorical depictions of fulfillment must suffice. But moving from song titles and utopian discourse to pragmatic moral fulfillments is not easy. Moreover, we are not sure of what to believe in anymore. We want justice, but what kind of justice do we want? In what kind of justice do we believe?

Those who survived Jim Crow, genocides of one type or another, and the violent interactions of the human family around issues of race, gender, and sexuality want to believe that the community-called-beloved is either selling lots for development or at least seeking zoning approval to demarcate its boundaries. We are committed and we are brave, yet racism and its "anti" tropes not only survive, they thrive. We don't believe in it, we verbally resist it, and we affirm its narrative opposite, but the reconciled community that we seek is locked in dream discourse while racism's tentacles grasp, cling, and anchor.

The search for a complete end to conflict is a daunting task. Why not begin on a more manageable level? Perhaps we can start by answering one question. Is there a response to Rodney King's plaintive question of the 1990s, "Can we all just get along?" Perhaps one response is that we have no basis for "getting along" that matches our learned rhetoric of victimization and dominance. Instead, we have mental reference

---

6. Dyson, *I May Not Get There*, 29.

points that situate ethnic and cultural communities along a continuum of aversion/attraction. We also have our beloved stereotypes.

In North America, it is a commonly held belief that black and Hispanic teens are more violent than Asian and white teens. Yet recent outbreaks of school violence seem to be concentrated in white suburban communities and recent mass shootings have been committed by white nationalists. Similar myths about the color of poverty persist despite statistical proof to the contrary. Today, racist discourse and assumptions are unlinked from racist actions in such a way that people seem confused as to the causes of ethnic-racial-sexual violence in society.

In fact, most of the overt metaphors for inferiority have become subliminal responses and reactions that can no longer be traced. As a result, incidents such as the murder of unarmed young people of color (POC), racial profiling by police departments and federal officers nationwide, Nazi protests in Charlottesville, and the voting harassment of black citizens throughout the US seem to have erupted out of nowhere.

At this point, I am addressing race in isolation from the tri-modal grid of oppression, even though I support the liberationist theory that race, class, and gender are interrelated concepts that cannot be addressed in isolation. From a philosophical perspective, phenomenologist Alfred Schütz noted there is no such thing as an isolated problem; issues impinge and overlap.[7]

Ralph Ellison makes the same point in his cultural essay *Shadow and Act*. He says that the problems of the African American community are the problems of the wider society. They are inextricably bound to one another.[8] Any problem is a problem within a context; it carries along its outer horizons references to other problems.[9] Race turns out to be a busy and complicated intersection of social locations that have an impact on and contribute to our conflicted responses to one another.

---

7. See discussion in Schütz, *Collected Papers 2*, 104, 105.

8. Ralph Ellison, *Shadow and Act* (New York: Vintage, 1972), 253.

9. Schütz, "Equality and the Meaning Structure of the Social World," in *Collected Papers 2*, 235.

The Idolatrous Cult of "Whiteness"

The planet reels from centuries of trying to make it light and white, fast, packaged, and marketable.[10]

THE COST OF SUCH an effort is a cult of whiteness that renders people invisible. Immediately after slavery, black people in America lived in a way that required virtual invisibility, secret keeping, and isolation. Today, migrant workers and refugees maintain a similar anonymity. The amazing thing about invisibility is that it cloaks both ends of the social spectrum. Euro-Americans who participated in or benefited from systems of oppression suffer from a similar syndrome. They also become invisible, but in different ways.

When "whiteness" is deemed to be normative, people who identify as "white" can't describe what it means to be categorized by their color. The whiteness that privileges also becomes a smothering gloss that eliminates individuality and awareness of self and others. Film professor Richard Dyer, in his intriguing study of whiteness, makes a salient point:

> As long as race is something only applied to non-white peoples, as long as white people are not racially seen and named, they/we function as a human norm. Other people are raced, we are just people. There is no more powerful position than that of being "just" human. The claim to power is the claim to speak for the commonality of humanity. Raced people can't do that—they can only speak for their race.[11]

The claim to neutral humanness bequeaths a position of superiority over most social systems (media, finance, and politics). The position is so powerful that it is maintained even when the real basis for "whiteness" is exposed. The confusion begins when whites claim that they have given

---

10. Larry L. Rasmussen, *Earth Community, Earth Ethics* (Maryknoll, NY: Orbis, 1996), 223.

11. Richard Dyer, *White: Essays on Race and Culture* (New York: Routledge, 1997), 1–2. See also Richard Dyer, *White: Twentieth Anniversary Edition* (New York: Routledge, 2017).

up their ethnicity in favor of nationalism. Most identify as un-hyphenated Americans. They may be Italian, Greek, or Irish, but allegiance is to American society. They wonder why African Americans, Native Americans, Asians, and Hispanics maintain their ethnic identifications. While the debate rages, few notice the silent retention of the most important identification—whiteness![12]

The truth of the matter is that there are no "white people." The immigrants from Europe that I referenced in the previous paragraph were not describe as "white" before they came to America. There is no continent or nation called "white" and there is only one human race. "Whiteness" is a category of social privilege that uses white skin as the identifying ticket of admission.

This admission to overt and subliminal power requires abandonment of ethnic specificity. Idolatrous whiteness also fears displacement and denies the diversity that is a natural order in our life space. In quantum and cosmological terms, diversity is normal. In the Western canon, it is not. Instead, it offers a story of conquest and the subjugation of others.

It was never the story of the many nations assembled in one geo-cultural location; rather, it has become the revisionist story of whiteness, one that can be told, but one that need not obliterate the other stories.

The idolatrous cult of whiteness is also articulated as a theological obsession with light as the only indicator of holiness. Religious symbols and languages have taught us that light is blessed and darkness is demonic, an unfortunate turn of events, as darkness is as complex and unique as any other event of the cosmos.

There is a darkness that opposes the light, rejects the power of divine transformation, and attempts to extinguish the hope and promise that are the forerunners of the *basileia* of God. There is a darkness that is the dwelling place of God, an enveloping comfort to the comforter, a place where the God consciousness can pause.

The phrase, "The world was dark and void" (Genesis 1:2) is not an indictment. It is an indication of the state of the universe in the beginning. In the beginning there is a natal darkness. It is the womb out of which we

12. Ibid., 4. See also David R. Roediger, *Working Toward Whiteness: How America's Immigrants Became White: The Strange Journey from Ellis Island to the Suburbs,* 2nd ed. (New York: Basic Books, 2018).

are born, a genesis space for "Let there be" and nurture. This is a mothering darkness that nurses its offspring. I am describing a darkness that is like rich loam, that strengthens us, encourages us to push deep roots into the dark earth, where we can grow toward the light fed by the darkness. There are still other darknesses that are yet to be revealed.

Judeo-Christian communities that predominate in North America have a faith legacy that recounts a beginning where darkness was dominant, yet we are still seduced by the light. Our religious discourses tout light as the evidence of God in our midst. Even though we are told that the evil one masquerades as an angel of light, and that God dwells in the welcoming darkness, we persist in this connection of light and white with goodness and holiness. The outcome is that those who live in dark skins become shadows in the world.

Dark Matter Matters

OUR PERSISTENT EQUATION of light with good and dark with evil belies a historical reality that provides another understanding.

> Because we get the symbols wrong, we get reality wrong. Light means life, we think, and darkness means foreboding, danger, death with all its authority. Yet since Hiroshima and Nagasaki, light has ghastly meanings, as it has since flames lit the night sky in the serene Polish countryside at Auschwitz.[13]

Rasmussen's discussion of the evil manifestations of light reminds us of how our visions of darkness are skewed and distorted. From a cosmological perspective, light is not what it seems. It is really energy/action, a form of electromagnetic radiation, visible to the human eye, that never rests or slows. It can be particle and wave, and we still do not understand this, but light is not the symbol of purity and static goodness implied in our theological discourses.

Our recoil from the dark refutes all protestations that race relations have changed. Dark people continue to represent pariahs and strangers in

13. Rasmussen, *Earth Community*, 220.

our midst. When W. E. B. Du Bois said that the color line is the problem of the twentieth century, all who heard it presumed that, like any wound, it would heal. It has not. We should not be surprised, since healing in this instance requires understanding, and we don't understand darkness or our responses to it.

When I discuss darkness, I am not referring exclusively to an ontological or physical trait. While darkness is tangibly embodied in dark people and in the universe, it can also be assigned as a marker of inferiority for those deemed to be of a lower-class status. The rap music genre captures the elusiveness of this assignment in the term "wigger." At the time that this term was popular, wiggers (a variation of the "N" word) were white children who were modeling the dress, discourse, and behavior of black rap artists.

The term inferred facile appropriations of inferiority that could be donned as a temporary musical fad. For white teens who bear the safe and permanent designation of "human," such excursions to the "dark side" can be thrilling. It also satisfies an abiding curiosity about the "dark" culture that dominance spends so much time and energy opposing.

Poor whites in economically depressed areas are also assigned a social status that marks them as completely as African Americans. They are allowed the designation "white," but often carry a linked negative image in the connecting term "trash." The fluidity of the assignment of darkness or denigrated concepts of whiteness does not empty the concept of its malignant effects. However, it does disclose the arbitrary and negotiable character of blackness and white purity in North American contexts.

According to cultural theorist Aaron David Gresson III,

> The painful irony is that "Blackness" has always been negotiable. Thus, the double bind: one really ought to let "Blackness" go, and one really ought to "be ashamed" to give it up so readily after all that "Blacks" have given to make the folly and lie a palatable reality. This is the ultimate sham and shamefulness of oppression: one will be "politically incorrect" whatever decision one ultimately makes.[14]

14. Aaron David Gresson III, *The Recovery of Race in America* (Minneapolis: University of Minnesota Press, 1995), 169. See also, by the same author, *America's Atone-*

It is Gresson's belief that postmodern societies generate folly and lies. He relies on rhetorical proofs found in terms such as "reverse racism."

The hatred of darkness is not just a discourse between dominant and oppressed communities; it is also the language of rejection in inter- and intra-cultural rhetoric. Geo-cultural theorist Yi-Fu Tuan points out that "a color can acquire a hideous vividness through the lens of hate. Hate attends to detail in a way disturbingly like that of love."[15]

As North America continues to diversify with the influx of new immigrants, worth and value continue to be assigned in ways that stratify people according to color and ethnic origin. Such stratifications foster new resentments between Asian, Hispanic, and Africana communities. These resentments are foolish given our common cosmological origins.

Scientists believe that the universe erupted out of an infinitesimally small pinhole, perhaps a black hole, but, in the beginning, there was no light, no time, only darkness. We are learning that we are all creatures of light and dark, living in a universe that is predominantly dark: current estimations state that 27 percent is dark matter, 68 percent is dark energy, and 5 percent is observable matter.[16]

Introducing a Dark Universe

JUST AS CORNEL WEST reminded us that race matters, the new physics and cosmology teach us that dark matter matters. A brief summary of the history of dark matter is necessary to understand fully the power and cultural potential of its language and descriptions. "Astronomers were … surprised and disturbed to learn in the 1930s that our own Milky Way galaxy behaved as if it contained more matter than could be seen with telescopes. This puzzling non-luminous matter became known as 'dark matter.'"[17]

ment: *Racial Pain, Recovery Rhetoric, and the Pedagogy of Healing*, 2nd ed. (New York: Peter Lang, 2015).

15. Tuan, *Passing Strange*, 12.

16. NASA Science, "Dark Energy, Dark Matter," https://science.nasa.gov/astrophysics/focus-areas/what-is-dark-energy, accessed September 1, 2019.

17. Nigel Smith and Neil Spooner, "The Search for Dark Matter," *Physics World* 13, no. 1 (January 2000): 1.

Vera Rubin (1928–2016), a student of the noted physicist Richard Feynman (1918–1988), was one of the pioneers in the study of dark matter. Indeed, her entire career was one of proposing ideas that challenged and questioned the status quo. Her master's thesis, written in 1951, suggested that the centripetal accelerations of galaxies might be caused by the gravitational effects of unseen matter. Her ideas were criticized because they raised questions about the big bang theory and its model of an expanding universe. Nevertheless, Rubin went on to receive her doctorate from Georgetown University. Her work with dark matter began after she joined the Department of Terrestrial Magnetism, which is part of the Carnegie Institution of Washington.[18]

In collaboration with Kent Ford, Rubin began to study the rotations of galaxies with a spectrograph. She expected that the mass closest to the center would rotate faster than the outer edges of a galaxy. Instead, she found that the outer edges of galaxies traveled as fast at the center, yet the system did not fly apart. Recalling the work of Fritz Zwicky (1898–1974) in the 1930s, who said that there had to be "missing mass" that was gluing the universe together, Rubin identified that mass as dark matter, because it was light and not mass that was missing. The discovery meant that astronomers had only seen a small portion of the universe.

But what is dark matter? Some scientists are reluctant to describe a phenomenon that is still quite mysterious. Others say it is like a cohesive but invisible material that sheds no detectable light. We know it is there because of the rotation of spiral galaxies like the Milky Way and the measurement of its mass. Dark matter may serve a vital function in the life of the universe if it is as powerful and connective as scientists presume. Thus far, analogies come closest to describing its effects.

Rubin stated that it could be like any other ordinary material such as

18. Rubin's observations were published as "Rotation of the Andromeda Nebula from a Spectroscopic Survey of Emissions Regions" with W. Kent Ford, Jr., *Astrophysical Journal* 159:379 (1970). See also Marcia Bartusiak, *Through a Universe Darkly: A Cosmic Tale of Ancient Ethers, Dark Matter, and the Fate of the Universe* (New York: HarperCollins, 1993); Rafi Letzter, "4 Dark Matter Searches to Watch in 2019," *Live Science*, January 1, 2019, https://www.livescience.com/64379-dark-matter-discoveries-2019.html; and Johns Hopkins University, "Dark Matter May Be Older than the Big Bang," *ScienceDaily*, August 7, 2019, https://www.sciencedaily.com/releases/2019/08/190807190816.htm.

cold gas, dust, or small black holes. It could be a category of dark objects called massive astrophysical compact halo objects (MACHOs) that are invisible but present in the halos of the galaxies. Today, most scientists think that dark matter is composed of non-baryonic matter. The leading candidate, weakly interacting massive particles (WIMPs), have ten to a hundred times the mass of a proton, but their weak interactions with "normal" matter make them difficult to detect.[19]

Clearly, dark matter is something that we don't understand and can't observe, or perhaps we don't understand gravity as well as we thought. However the dark elements of the universe are described, they are assumed to be powerful and predominant. My point here is that the universe confirms our common origins and interconnections. However, those who persist in games of white dominance should be forewarned that the new physics and cosmology offer concepts that can be appropriated for similar claims of dominance by the two-thirds world.

Of course, the better option is for all of us to celebrate our commonalities and rejoice in our differences. In a culture where darkness has been deemed a harbinger of evil, a marker of inferiority, the opposite of all things good and virtuous, the unveiling of dark matter holds out the possibility of communal "conversion," a rhetorical turning to hopeful things.

In the place of discourses of inferiority and marginalization, dark matter is a symbol of power and relevance. It also offers dark people an opportunity to begin to see themselves as metaphorically connected to a darkness that is predominant in the universe. This darkness is vital to the future of the cosmos and necessary for its continuance. Even its invisibility can be appropriated as a gift that symbolizes healing that can permeate where words of apology can never reach.

The heavy particles that may be the substance of dark matter infuse the spirit and the body so that "a billion of them would be passing through your body every second, and yet you would not be able to detect them."[20]

19. Nola Taylor Redd, "What is Dark Matter?" *Space.com,* updated July 16, 2019, https://www.space.com/20930-dark-matter.html.

20. James Glanz, quoting particle physicist Dr. Leszek Roszkowski, "Evidence of Mystery Particles Stirring Excitement and Doubt," *New York Times*, Science Section, February 19, 2000, https://www.nytimes.com/2000/02/19/world/evidence-of-mystery-particles-stirring-excitement-and-doubt.html.

This healing element cannot be discounted, given Cornel West's statement that nihilism is a disease of the soul that recurs and can seldom be cured. Perhaps the cure lies beyond the boundaries of our current knowledge or in the mystery of spinning galaxies.

In the place of discourses of inferiority and marginalization, dark matter can be a symbol of cosmic power that offers dark people an opportunity to see themselves as metaphorically connected to a darkness that is predominant in the universe. Darkness is vital to the future of our universe and necessary for its continuance. But is dark matter in every galaxy? Recent discoveries indicate that there may be places in the cosmos where it does not exist.

In recent years, scientists have confirmed a galaxy located some sixty million light-years away, named NGC 1052-DF2 (DF2), that has no discernible dark matter. Astronomer Peter van Dokkum of Yale University led the team that discovered DF2. While they were trying to verify their initial findings, another dim and diffuse galaxy with a lack of dark matter was found and nicknamed DF4.

> Taken together, the new papers show DF2 is not alone, but instead part of a larger and previously unknown population of galaxies that have seemingly freed themselves from the bonds of dark matter. This new research may have dramatic implications for prevailing theories about the formation and evolution of galaxies, as well as the true nature of dark matter itself.[21]

Dark Energy

WE HAVE BEEN AWARE, ever since the big bang theory was announced, that the universe is expanding. It was also presumed that gravity would affect that expansion and possibly slow it down in some respects. Efforts to measure that expansion have led to another astounding find. Instead of a gradual slowdown, the pedal is to the metal and the universe is speeding

21. Jake Parks, "Second Ghostly Galaxy without Dark Matter Discovered, First Confirmed," *Astronomy*, March 29, 2019, https://astronomy.com/news/2019/03/ghostly-galaxy-without-dark-matter-confirmed.

up. Scientists believe that antigravity or dark energy is responsible. What is it? "It is a property of empty space that exerts an outward force like a compressed spring at every point in space."[22]

Some scientists predict that there is the same amount of dark energy between galaxies. The effect of this balance is that when the distance between galaxies widens, the force of dark energy increases exponentially, pushing the galaxies away from one another with an ever-increasing force. Other scientists think that dark energy has the properties of anti-matter and that it has overwhelmed gravity in ways that will cause the universal expansion to increase at faster and faster rates.[23]

All things being equal, a universe that is out of balance will eventually fly apart. A society in the same state with respect to justice will come to the same end. The scientists who describe dark energy as a coiled spring believe that it exerts doubled forces when increasing distances separate entities in the universe. Could the same forces be operative in the cultural realm? Could our affinities for separation and distance from one another uncoil the spring that sends us reeling in ways that are catastrophic and final?

The metaphors of power that can be drawn from scientific concepts of dark matter and dark energy can help all people to re-envision darkness in ways that transcend inferiority and denigration. How marvelous it would be if all children of every culture viewed darkness as a symbol of connectedness, with equal power and intensity of light in a universe that requires both.

Dark Flow

TO MAKE THINGS even more interesting, in 2010, NASA reported a theory that describes dark flow.

> Distant galaxy clusters mysteriously stream at a million miles per hour along a path roughly centered in the southern constellations Centaurus and Hydra. A new study led by Alexander Kashlinsky at NASA's Goddard Space Flight Center in Greenbelt, MD, tracks this

---

22. Michael D. Lemonick, "Einstein's Repulsive Idea," *Time* (April 16, 2001): 58.
23. Ibid.

collective motion—dubbed the "dark flow"—to twice the distance originally reported.[24]

According to Princeton cosmologist J. Richard Gott, dark flow may be an indication that we live in a multiverse, where the laws of physics may permit the universe to be its own mother.[25]

While theories are fascinating, all we can conclude at this point is that darkness is a power in our universe. From a rhetorical perspective, we are observing a trinity of darknesses: dark energy, dark matter, and dark flow. Dark energy seems to be accelerating the expansion of the universe, dark matter seems to be a holding mechanism of the cosmos, and dark flow may be the response of galactic objects to a force outside of this universe that is pulling them beyond the known realm. The mysteries abound.

Black Is Also Light

COSMOLOGY TEACHES US that "whiteness" is not the only analogy that complements the light. In fact, as physicist Stephen Hawking (1942–2018) noted, "black holes ain't that black."[26] To be able to reconfigure our ideas about darkness, we must be willing to accept fluid definitions. Whereas the idea of dark matter offers a rhetorical response to the idolatry of whiteness as a cult of superiority, black holes connect darkness to the light. "Black holes are the result of stars collapsing in on themselves due to the depletion of hydrogen and other gasses. But they are not *black*;

---

24. J. Richard Gott and Li-Xin Li, "Can the Universe Create Itself?" *Physical Review D* 58 (1998), https://doi.org/10.1103/PhysRevD.58.023501. See also recent articles discussing dark flow, including NASA/Goddard Space Flight Center, "Mysterious Cosmic 'Dark Flow' Tracked Deeper into Universe," *Science Daily*, March 11, 2010, https://www.sciencedaily.com/releases/2010/03/100310162829.htm.

25. Sophie Weiner, "Are Galaxies Flowing Toward a Point Beyond Our Universe?" *Popular Mechanics*, August 4, 2017, https://www.popularmechanics.com/space/deep-space/a27635/dark-flow-space-time/. See also Maggie McKee, "Blow for 'Dark Flow' in Planck's New View of the Cosmos," *New Scientist*, April 3, 2013, https://www.newscientist.com/article/dn23340-blow-for-dark-flow-in-plancks-new-view-of-the-cosmos/.

26. Crosley, *The Vodou Quantum Leap*, 76.

in fact, they are *white hot*."[27] Scientists speculate that black holes may be the birth site of the universe. The energy and gravitational pull exerted is extraordinary.

Imagine a cosmos born out of blackness that is also light. Under such circumstances, color loses its false social indicators. Moreover, wormholes may connect through black holes to parallel universes. Such speculation would make black holes conduits to other realities. Recent scientific probes indicate that there may be black holes at the center of every galaxy, some actively feeding, others spent by the process of evaporation and explosion. The possibilities for symbolic and metaphoric appropriations are stunning.

In April of 2019, we saw the silhouette of a black hole for the first time. Scientists using the Event Horizon Telescope observed it at the center of the galaxy M87. They said, "The image shows a bright ring formed as light bends in the intense gravity around a black hole that is 6.5 billion times more massive than the sun."[28]

> Black holes, with their incredible gravitational pull, are basically time machines. Get on a rocket, travel to Sagittarius A*...
> For every minute you spend there, a thousand years will pass on Earth. It's hard to believe, but that's what happens. Gravity trumps time.[29]

A black hole is a power that not even light can escape and, as Finkel states, it can bend time. I have a feeling that Sojourner Truth, Thich Nhat Hanh, Huey P. Newton, Mahatma Gandhi, and Stokely Carmichael would not be surprised by the secrets that the cosmos is revealing.

---

27. O'Murchu, *Quantum Theology*, 125.

28. Ota Lutz, "How Scientists Captured the First Image of a Black Hole," *NASA / Jet Propulsion Laboratory*, April 19, 2019, https://www.jpl.nasa.gov/edu/news/2019/4/19/how-scientists-captured-the-first-image-of-a-black-hole/.

29. Michael Finkel, "Star Eater," *National Geographic*, March 2014, https://www.nationalgeographic.com/magazine/2014/03/black-holes-einstein-star-eaters/.

Racial Progress and Special Relativity

THERE ARE TWO theories of relativity: general and special. The general theory says that "the shape of space *responds* to objects in the environment. . . . The agent of gravity, according to Einstein, is the fabric of the cosmos."[30] Imagine a trampoline with a heavy rock or bowling ball in its center; the warping of the fabric caused by the weight of the objects is similar to the warping of space-time by planetary systems. The difference, of course, is that space-time has more dimensions than a trampoline, so the warping is on all sides and also affects the path of light.

I am suggesting that weight/mass is not just a physical phenomenon but also a spiritual state of being. Like planets and stars, we are also moving through this space fabric, bending and warping the life space. Our movements affect the cosmos and the direction of light; our decisions and actions have effects on others. All of our communities and ecosystems are necessary; nothing is expendable in a universe where deep impressions are made.

General relativity tells us that space-time changes in relation to matter and, in physicist Brian Greene's estimation, it may actually tear and mend in ways that change both the topology and topography of space.[31] General relativity affects massive objects; special relativity comes into play when movement is discussed. The main premise of special relativity is that "observers in relative motion will have different perceptions of distance and of time."[32]

The effects of special relativity are not apparent unless you are traveling "at a substantial fraction of light speed."[33] We have all experienced relative motion when we ride in one vehicle and see another passing. Under such circumstances, we have no adequate means to determine our motion. Nor can we experience the disparities of time in relative motion.

---

30. Greene, *The Elegant Universe*, 69, 71. See also "Brian Greene Introduces the Theory of General Relativity," *World Science Festival*, December 14, 2014, https://www.youtube.com/watch?v=oHnaLnUdYvs.

31. Paul S. Aspinwall, Brian R. Greene, and David R. Morrison, "Multiple Mirror Manifolds and Topology Change in String Theory," in *Physics Letters* B 303 (3–4): 249–259, April 1993.

32. Greene, *The Elegant Universe*, 25.

33. Ibid.

It seems that "time elapses more slowly for an individual in motion than it does for a stationary individual."[34] This fact has interesting implications. Greene says that, in the microworld, muons die if stationary, but have their life expectancies extended when they are traveling through a particle accelerator.[35] He states that the same would be true for humans if they could move as quickly as muons. The metaphysical turn is obvious. Movement sustains and enhances life, but those who are in motion feel as if time is passing more slowly.

We cannot discern differences of time without accelerations in speed that do not normally occur in daily life. It is not that time differentials do not occur; it's that we can't perceive them. Those who have been seeking justice are impatient with the rate of progress when, in fact, progress may be occurring in ways that are not easily discernible. But the idea of progress may be as antiquated as medieval ideas about the universe.

People moving in relation to one another have different perspectives on progress, and each has a claim to truth. In "Letter from a Birmingham Jail," Martin Luther King, Jr. addressed these varying perspectives of space-time.[36] To well-meaning white clergy, gradualism seemed adequate, but to those subject to hangings, castrations, and psychic annihilation, "soon and very soon" was the only acceptable timetable. Moving in relation to one another, the timing seemed too fast from one perspective and too slow from another. To redeem the time, King appropriated the language of the gospel and the already/not yet *basileia* of God.

The other consequence of this movement in space-time is that the past is with us but without constraints. The past is a point of reference, a place to which we can return for a reconsideration of history, but it is not behind us. It is with us in the present and the future because, according to Einstein's theory of special relativity, time is relative.

Accordingly, the pain of the past may also be our future; the hope of the future may be available right now.

---

34. Ibid., 41.

35. Ibid., 42.

36. Martin Luther King, Jr., "Letter from a Birmingham Jail," April 16, 1963, https://www.africa.upenn.edu/Articles_Gen/Letter_Birmingham.html.

Omnicentricity:
Who's In, Who's Out

THE IDEA THAT the universe is expanding changes everything. How can we continue to talk about cultural centers and margins when the new cosmology teaches that the universe is expanding in a very odd way? Rather than a universe that expands from one point, the universe contains multiple centers that are expanding at the same time. I have no doubt that there are formulaic ways to express this idea, but I will try to work within the limits of language.

Omnicentricity means that all centers act as focal points for the activity of expansion and energy. This makes every center special, and it certainly makes expansion an event.[37] In a world of simultaneously expanding centers, there are no margins. The language of margins belongs to mechanistic ideas of a clockwork universe. Understanding this idea of multiple centers might change the discourse of race.

We might be able to stop the struggle to determine who's on top, whose numbers in the latest census indicate that they are the minority to court—the minority of the future. It might also limit the language of victimization. Even the most malignant forces of domination cannot hold down a community that is cosmically on the move. Seekers of justice marched to offer a visual picture of emancipation to those who were deluded into thinking that chains mattered, and because social constructs can neither define nor confine the human spirit.

The language of "being held down" is part of the delusional web that closes the portal to the future. Once again, I rely upon Brian Swimme. He says, "Where we are situated, we are at the center of the expansion, but we are also at the periphery from someone else's point of view."[38] If everything is moving, then the struggles for justice are also movement, whether or not they are as fast, effective, or efficient as we would like.

---

37. Swimme, "The Universe Story as Sacred Story," 140.
38. Ibid., 141.

A Fly in the Buttermilk:
Integration from a Cosmological Perspective

THE MOVEMENT OF every center means that, on a deeper level, one cannot integrate. One can coincide, separate, or even collide. Integration has an aura of stasis. I must resort to a cooking metaphor to clarify my thoughts. Often, when we bake a cake, the batter has something else folded into it. The image of a marble cake comes to mind, wherein chocolate and vanilla are swirled together. But even this isn't integration so much as it is enfolding, for the dark streaks remain distinct, even in the pale batter. Integration requires that systems devised for survival be abandoned for the privilege of being included in the batter. Yet, like the ancestors always said, you can always find the "fly in the buttermilk." For African Americans, color defined and separated, while darkness carried with it markers of inferiority that could not be suppressed.

Today, physicists are looking for the theory of everything (TOE) that will unite all of the forces in the universe. Perhaps it was not integration that we needed, but a cultural theory of everything (CTOE), a guiding principle that would combine our differing proclivities to move and struggle and create—a notion that would value differentials of time, mass, and power.

Those who have the mass/weight/power can warp the space-time matrix in ways that affect the trajectory of light, but those who are invisible and necessary hold the cosmos together. Uniting all the cultural forces of the world will require respect for difference and darkness. This cultural theory of everything brings me to a discussion of the incredible vibrating strings that may be the elemental foundations of the universe.

String Theory:
For It Does Not Yet Appear as It Shall Be

AS IT TURNS OUT, the elders knew what they were talking about. The universe is rhythmic and vibrant. The quantum world is filled with tiny strings, "whose vibrational patterns orchestrate the evolution of the cosmos."[39] Physicists now hypothesize that "all matter and all forces…

39. Greene, *The Elegant Universe*, 135. See also Ani Ananthaswamy, "Found: A

arise from one basic ingredient: oscillating strings."[40] As Brian Greene explains, strings vibrate and create resonances that give rise to varying forces, charges, and masses. When we view the world around us and its constituent properties, we may be viewing the "notes" that strings play.[41]

Leonard Susskind, one of the founders of string theory, now says that diversity may be the key to explaining baffling features of our universe. While scientists are looking for one elegant, verifiable law of physics that applies to the entire cosmos, they are finding just the opposite. They are finding that different laws of physics may apply in different universes. The elegance is found in the creativity and diversity of the cosmos.[42]

If strings are the foundational element of matter, they would comprise all aspects of nature, including human bodies and distant stars. Just as a musical note vibrates when played, strings resonating in varied modes may represent the concrete elements of the universe.

The differences that we see in a complex world may be vibrational differences—one resonance for plant life, another for human. However, because variations emerge from the quantum realm, the differences that strings create are not immutable or hierarchical, but an étude or sonata from the cosmos to us.

Difference can then be viewed as variation on a theme. What we shall be has not yet appeared, because images of physical embodiment don't subsume human potential. Although people appear to be black, white, or brown; gay, straight, or bi; male or female; able or differently abled; these are resonances that reflect a universe that appreciates and solicits difference.

Sexuality, gender, class, and race are not deterministic categories; rather, they are fugues and études in a larger and more complex symphony. As a consequence, those who exhibit particular ways of embodiment should be neither assigned static moral value nor divested of it. We are

Quadrillion Ways for String Theory to make our Universe," *Scientific American,* March 28, 2019, https://www.scientificamerican.com/article/found-a-quadrillion-ways-for-string-theory-to-make-our-universe/.

40. Greene, *The Elegant Universe,* 136.

41. Ibid., 16.

42. Ker Than, "A Cosmic Symphony of Vibrating Strings," *Stanford News,* September 11, 2018, https://news.stanford.edu/2018/09/11/cosmic-symphony-vibrating-strings/.

RACE AND THE COSMOS

beings of light and dark and difference. We are dying and transcending death. The complexities seem almost musical to scientists. Perhaps this is a salient hint. These ideas are more than we can *say*, but not, perhaps, more than we can *sing*.

Summary

WE MAY HAVE to revisit our past, but it does not bind us. Although the past may be a point of reference for pain or blame, in an expanding universe, we are all free to become manifestations of our ancestors' hopes and our children's dreams. As it turns out, we are not working toward integration or incorporation or any other grand teleological narrative, but rather the dual transformation of dominant and insurgent groups. This process is one that will require the continued renegotiation of narrative, cultural, educational, and sacred space.[43] These are tasks worthy of our energy and focus.

.

43. See Barry Kanpol and Peter McLaren, eds, *Critical Multiculturalism: Uncommon Voices in a Common Struggle* (Westport, CT: Bergin & Garvey, 1995), 11.

six

∷

Ultimate reality, whatever that turns out to be,
is the end of the quest. Paradoxically, it must also be the beginning.
We must ask whether there is anything about our universe,
about ourselves, that we can take for granted—
any fundamental we can use as a starting place
for the exploration of everything else.
If it is difficult to find such a "still point"—
and we shall find that it is indeed difficult—
then the quest for ultimate truth must begin with a leap of faith.
Not faith that we are capable of complete understanding.
Faith that we can know anything at all.

—Kitty Ferguson,
The Fire in the Equations: Science, Religion, and the Search for God

∷

We are fighting for an unapologetic movement for economic,
social, and racial justice in the United States.

—Alexandria Ocasio-Cortez

∷

That's all anybody can do right now. Live. Hold out. Survive.
I don't know whether good times are coming back again.
But I know that won't matter if we don't survive these times.

—Octavia Butler

∷

⁘ *6* ⁘

Quantum Contexts and Dominance

Anyone who is not shocked by quantum mechanics
has not understood it.
—Niels Bohr

Quantum mechanics is important for our psychological and spiritual
formation because it fatally undermines the deterministic character that
both science and theology had formerly imposed on nature.
—Angela Tilby, *Soul: God, Self, and the New Cosmology*

W E HAVE BEEN tilting at windmills. Our generational focus on the color line obscured the cause of our troubles. Because we assumed that racism was the sole cause of our cultural conflicts, we targeted most of our efforts toward creating a society that did not use "color" as a demarcation of inferiority. We now know that the discourse of black and white ignored the wide spectrum of ethnic groups that didn't fit into either category. But, more importantly, the focus on color masked our struggles for power.

This struggle for dominance did not just manifest itself in race relations. Difference in the form of gender, sexuality, and even ability received the same crushing opposition. According to those who wielded power, the God who delegated authority to run the world was neither female, gay, differently abled, nor ethnic. Once it was determined that an idolatrous and European depiction of God would be deemed normative, oppression of all others had to be the logical result. God's self-identification as a Spirit was treated as a mere suggestion and was replaced by an Anglo grandfatherly figure.

We want a god who looks and acts like us. We want our world to be solid, tactile, and within reach. Is it any wonder that we are comforted by James Weldon Johnson's poetic description of divine creativity? In his sermonic poem, an anthropomorphic God plows and treads mountains and valleys into existence and molds humankind into embodied companions in a tangible world.[1]

Science and theology supported this artistic description by describing accessible secular and spiritual realms. These images that we constructed of God's abode and ours conveniently left room for human domination and control. This chapter considers the latest developments in quantum physics from a cultural and philosophical perspective. It is an attempt to extrapolate new understandings about the nature of the universe, dominance, and oppression.[2]

At the beginning of this book, I spoke of the cries of distress echoing from both majority and minority communities. This is what I hear:

- The cry from previously dominant cultures is for some clue as to where stability can be found. There is the unspoken desire for a unifying ideal and a way to orient themselves toward difference without losing a sense of order.
- The cry from marginalized communities is for rootedness in timeless and universal truths about their human dignity. This desire does not abate with well-intentioned laws or the guarded beneficence of those who once controlled access to life itself.

1. James Weldon Johnson, *God's Trombones: Seven Negro Sermons in Verse* (New York: Viking, 1927).

2. There are excellent books available for those who desire further forays into the field of quantum physics. The only caution is that quantum physics is a dynamic area of study that is permeated with delightful uncertainties. In many cases, physicists are not sure of what their latest findings mean. Under such conditions, humility seems to be the best hermeneutic.

It has been my argument throughout this book that new perspectives on the nature of the life space and the universe enhance our collective understandings of self and society. If we can catch a glimpse of the false assumptions about dominance and human hierarchies, we have a reasonable hope of revising the script. The following discussion juxtaposes quantum theory with issues of dominance.

The Quantum Story:
Those Who Have Not Been Shocked Have Not Understood

BY THE END of the nineteenth century, Western civilization thought it had figured out the inner workings of the universe. It seemed that physics couldn't uncover anything new, and then another layer of information was received that displaced the latest theories.[3] Three important areas of inquiry emerged: mechanics, which is the study of force and motion; electromagnetism, which focuses on the attributes of light; and thermodynamics, which focuses on energy, its change from one form to another, and the properties of heat. Each area of interest presumed cause-and-effect relationships in a deterministic model.[4]

The quantum world doesn't work in that way. Quantum physics is the science of incredibly small subatomic bits of matter. Current knowledge is that strings or elementary particles like quarks and leptons may be the basic elements of the universe. Of course, this could change at any moment. The existence of those elements is inferred in mathematical formulations and experiments that require atomic colliders, but the movement of these particles can't be predicted or anticipated.

These "subatomic particles seem to participate in reality in a different way from objects that can be observed and measured by classical physics."[5] In the quantum world, electrons jump and leap without rhyme or reason and get more and more active if the space they are in diminishes. An

---

3. Here, I am following scientific writer Angela Tilby's excellent summary of the history of classical physics found in *Soul: God, Self and the New Cosmology*, cited earlier. My interpretation of scientific theory is for the purpose of gleaning cultural insights.

4. Tilby, *Soul*, 12.

5. Ibid., 18.

electron enclosed in a space that gets smaller will become increasingly erratic. Brian Greene states,

> You would find the electron getting more and more frantic. Almost as if it were overcome with claustrophobia, the electron will go increasingly haywire—bouncing off of the walls of the box with increasingly frenetic and unpredictable speed. Nature does not allow its constituents to be cornered.[6]

Yet, in cultural contexts, injustice corners people and dominance diminishes thriving life spaces and reorders priorities. Is it any wonder that teens from disintegrating families and communities under economic siege, for example, may react in ways that are deleterious to society? We are integral parts of the cosmos, and the cosmos doesn't want us cornered.

On the quantum level,

> Some of what happens . . . is extremely difficult to explain in a way that satisfies our wish for a common-sense description. . . . In the case of an individual elementary particle, [a] definite series of events, [a] definite history, is missing. . . . What it has is a blur of possible histories.[7]

I am reminded of the question that my students posed about their own attenuated links to the African continent. Like quantum particles, the life histories of Africans in the diaspora cannot be traced as a linear connection between ancestors. Rather, individual histories include a mix of experience, genetic coding, and historical memory. Our lineage is both spiritual and dynamic in ways that link all of us to the history of the universe.

As it turns out, quantum particles are also difficult to pin down. Elements in the quantum world have a chaotic existence and can be said to be both here and there. In the most enigmatic way, things pop in and out of existence. One wonders how anything so elusive can be useful in a cultural study. Upon closer analysis, it makes perfect sense to use something that is

---

6. Greene, *The Elegant Universe*, 114.

7. Kitty Ferguson, *The Fire in the Equations: Science, Religion, and the Search for God* (Grand Rapids: W. B. Eerdmans, 1995), 13, 15.

RACE AND THE COSMOS

difficult to grasp to unlock something that is difficult to grasp. The elusive discourses of quantum physics and cosmology may be the perfect tools to unlock the shadowy concepts of domination and victimization.

Social Location, Domination, and Victimization

THE TWENTIETH CENTURY ushered in an era of scientific advancements and the rhetoric of victimization and oppression. This binary rhetorical construct undergirded every social movement of the century. The language was welcomed as a refreshing and empowering alternative to passivity and self-hatred; however, it has proven to be a conceptual quagmire. At the beginning of the twenty-first century, we are still bound by cycles of blaming and guilt.

It is important to understand the concepts of domination and victimization. While this book began with a call for a sleepwalking populace to awaken to their connections to universal realities, social theorist Michel Foucault (1926–1984) offered another perspective. He argued that the struggle is not to awaken consciousness, but to drain power from those systems that exploit the human community.[8] This is a noble ambition, but one that is thwarted by confusion as to the locus and contours of domination and victimization. Like quantum particles, they are both here and there. Because abuse of power is so difficult to pin down, those who have been named as dominators can often shift the focus and declare themselves victims.

Cultural theorist Aaron David Gresson III notes the rhetorical reversals that confuse and fuel cultural conflicts. In his article entitled "White Recovery of Moral and Heroic Voice: How to Say 'Yo' Mama!' When You're Already the 'Man,'" Gresson defines rhetorical reversal as "the neutralization of a historical or factually based trope by the misuse of its moral power in relation to self."[9]

---

8. "A Conversation between Michel Foucault and Gilles Deleuze," *L'Arc* 49 (March 4, 1972): 3–10. See also Juliana Menasce Horowitz, Anna Brown, and Kiana Cox, "Race in America 2019," *Pew Research Center* Social and Demographic Trends, April 9, 2019, https://www.pewsocialtrends.org/2019/04/09/race-in-america-2019/.

9. Gresson, *The Recovery of Race*, 164.

This tactic (accompanied by moral outrage) allows those who wield power to describe themselves as victims. Gresson sees a particularly insidious pattern that includes redefining acts of dominance as individual responses that have no institutional underpinnings, taking control of meaning by depicting the victim as the "real" oppressor, and, finally, refusing to admit that current privilege is directly related to past exploitations.[10] When the media reinforces these rhetorical deceptions, it becomes almost impossible to refute the underlying premise.

The fact that the assertions are based on false constructs can't be easily exposed. If everyone publicly agrees that the emperor is wearing clothes, then the naked king can march down Main Street with impunity. Exploited persons often find themselves in the untenable position of having to deny and argue with false constructs.

However, education may offer a way out of this circular paradigm. The problem is that very few educational systems teach children about the history of dominance and victimization in the world. To do so would give a new generation the means necessary to recognize and combat the phenomenon.

Since the concepts of victimization and oppression seem to be crucial to the construct of domination, it seems appropriate here to define the ideas. "Victimization" is a word that encompasses the abuse and misuse of members of the human community, accompanied by the concomitant loss of self-definition. The word "oppression," in its common usage, refers to the exercise of power/tyranny over others.[11] Both words describe spiritual as well as physical states of being. In recent years, these definitions have evoked memories of colonization, conquest, apartheid, segregation, and xenophobia. Both racism and oppression evoke images of institutional enforcement and both are malleable enough to manifest in any number of ways.

I like Walter Wink's discussion of oppression and domination because it includes the spiritual dimension. He wrote that "domination is always more than a power relation.... It is a *spiritual state of being....* A

---

10. Ibid.

11. Iris Marion Young, "Five Faces of Oppression," in *Multiculturalism from the Margins: Non-Dominant Voices on Difference and Diversity*, ed. Dean A. Harris (Westport, CT: Bergin & Garvey, 1995), 66.

sense of powerlessness is always a spiritual disease deliberately induced by the Powers to keep us complicit."[12] Also, of course, this sense of power-lessness speaks to the lack of decision-making power and self-esteem that becomes part of the reality of exploited persons.

Given the intrinsic relationality of the universe, it is safe to conclude that human forces of domination and their institutional counterparts exist in estrangement from God, self, society, and the universe. This is not to say that power is intrinsically evil. Wink reminded us that Jesus "does not reject power, but only its use to dominate others."[13] Power is to be used to enhance relationships, to identify with those who are rejected, and to empower those who are powerless.

Any discussion of power should begin with an explanation of the usage of the word. However, the act of defining is, in itself, an exercise of power. There are many theories of power set forth in the writings of Michel Foucault, Jacques Derrida, James Cone, bell hooks, and others. I prefer to explicate power through narratives. Through stories, we know what power does and how it makes us feel when we use, abuse, or lack it.

Power exists on every side of an issue; imbalance occurs when a party or group cedes all options to the other. When the Civil Rights movement began, segregationists had power, but they didn't have enough power to stop the impetus of justice. The marchers had power, but not enough to change the hearts of their opponents.

I want to describe a narrative model of power taken from the ser-monic wisdom of the Reverend Gardner Taylor (1918–2015). On the occasion of the thirtieth anniversary of the death of Martin Luther King, Jr., Taylor came to Memphis, Tennessee, where I taught ethics and Afri-can American religious studies.

During his sermon, he asked this question: "How did the descen-dants of slaves become the benchmark for a nation's direction?" Leaving this question for the listener to answer, Taylor began a description of parallel hierarchies of power found in the third chapter of Luke. In this text, nations and religious systems are undermined at the most unlikely moments by the God who will not restrain us from mistreating one

---

12. Wink, *Engaging the Powers*, 101, 103.
13. Ibid., 111.

another and who will not remain within the confines of our carefully articulated theologies. Taylor said:

> In the fifteenth year of the reign of Tiberius Caesar, Pontius Pilate being the governor of Judea seated in the seat of judgment with the seal of Rome over his head, Herod being the Oriental monarch, and Annas and Caiaphas being the high priests of Israel, wearing the purple robes and the miter of God, the Word of God (read power) came to John the Baptist in the wilderness.
>
> In the year that Dwight D. Eisenhower was president, in a nation with the mechanized power of armies and the financial power of Wall Street, John Patterson being the governor of Alabama, J. Edgar Hoover being the ominous head of the FBI, Norman Vincent Peale being the high priest of middle America, the Word of God (read power) came to Martin King in the wilderness of America.[14]

I take it from Taylor's lyrical analogy that the reality of power, though analyzed, circumscribed, and autopsied, will manifest itself in undetermined ways. Like quantum elements, only probabilities can be ascertained, and an incredible amount of power can be contained in small and unlikely places.

The defining aspect of quantum elements is the inability to predict outcomes. We have witnessed similar uncertainties in recent history. Through the most unlikely of circumstances, the Berlin Wall fell, Nelson Mandela survived imprisonment, and a southern Baptist preacher from Georgia changed the direction of a nation.

It is as if the universe is trying to recreate the balances that were lost by human manipulations of the social order and physical realm. Although people battle and struggle to gain power, it is often achieved in the most unlikely ways. But what is power in a world that is not of our making? We have no answers about our beginning or ending. Under such circumstances, how can power be anything other than an illusion that allows us to construct a framework for our activities?

Science also offers power, "but, as so often happens when people

---

14. Gardner Taylor, "Tribute to Martin Luther King, Jr.," sermon given during the "Pilgrimage to Memphis," Memphis, Tennessee, April 1998.

are seduced by promises of power, the price is servitude and impotence. Power is nothing if it is not the power to choose."[15] Power that is granted or gifted is an unstable appendage that can't be sustained over any period of time.

Sometimes, power differentials equalize when the stories of the excluded become as normative as those of the majority. It is important to see oneself and one's community reflected within shared histories. When I taught slave religion at Memphis Theological Seminary, some of the older students were stunned to find their recollections in course texts. They were even more surprised to realize that their memories of sewing underwear from crocus sacks, picking cotton in Mississippi, knowing the difference between buttermilk and clabber milk, sitting on moaner's benches, listening to the unique sounds of sacred harp, or singing by shape notes are valued in religious education.

Michel Foucault offered another perspective on the issue of domination. He argued that oppression can occur and be sustained by unsuspecting people whose choices, purchases, and educational processes contribute to the devaluing of others. Well-meaning people would immediately ask, "What does oppression look like in these contexts so that we can avoid, dismantle, and reject it?"

Social theorist Iris Marion Young (1949–2006) set forth five categories of oppression: exploitation, marginalization, powerlessness, cultural imperialism, and violence. I am adding my own category of cosmic myopia, which takes into account the influence of science on the discussion.[16] Young identified the modalities of oppression using a Marxist class analysis to argue that only a restructuring of the market forces and its reigning ideology can change social tendencies toward exploitation.

Young deemed marginalization to be "the most dangerous form of oppression," because its territory is broader.[17] She noted that people are marginalized by virtue of age, sexuality, race, gender, and ethnicity. It is a process that excludes some people from participation in the social schema.

---

15. Joseph Weizenbaum, *Computer Power and Human Reason: From Judgment to Calculation* (San Francisco: Freeman, 1976), 1273.

16. Young, "Five Faces." Here, I am summarizing Young's categories of oppression found on pages 72–86.

17. Ibid., 77.

This is a familiar social description that does not take into account the scientific theory of Omnicentricity that centers each living being.

Margins aren't relevant concepts in this theory. Instead, each of us exists in a center or sphere of reference and relationships that cannot be redefined by systems of domination. Theologian C. S. Lewis (1898–1963) agreed: "There seems [to be] no plan because it is all plan: there seems [to be] no center because it is all center."[18] If we take the findings of quantum physics seriously, the language of marginalization and its effects will be discarded.

Cultural imperialism is also named as a particularly virulent form of oppression that imposes a worldview in ways that denigrate and eliminate other perspectives. To maintain this hegemony, dominant cultures will sometimes include designated ethnic groups in their definition of normalcy. In North America, I have found that this inclusion strategy offers honorary Anglo status to some and not others.

The effects pit one ethnic group against another—for example, Asians against blacks, blacks against Hispanics. The struggle among diverse cultures for primacy reflects a view of the universe that is completely hierarchical. The quantum world refutes this assumption and induces us to accept a space that allows growth and mutuality.

Finally, Young recognized oppression in the form of systematic violence. Who can deny the existence of irrefutable power when one group has the ability to harm and kill other groups with impunity? Sometimes the violence occurs as implicitly sanctioned state/institutional action (executions, war, police shootings of unarmed young people of color, and imprisonment) or erratic individual behavior (hangings, personal and public violence against ethnic minorities, or rape). Usually, harm comes to those who don't have the power to resist or who fall through the economic cracks in such catastrophic ways that they must devise survival systems that run counter to social norms.

These categories, though insightful, do not cover all the types and expressions of oppression. One category that is missing is cosmic myopia. I define this as an exclusive focus on closed social and religious systems that negate options for freedom and limit our awareness of intrinsic and cosmic connections. People who are conscious of their connections

18. C. S. Lewis, *Perelandra* (New York: Macmillan, 1946), 229.

to the cosmos will not be deterred from full exploration of their gifts, because true liberation includes the ability to conceptualize freedom beyond social configuration.

Although freedom is difficult to conceive or embrace when fixed determinatives predominate, quantum physics speaks in a very different way about location and determinism. One of the best examples comes from the Heisenberg uncertainly principle.

The Uncertainty Principle

IN 1927, WERNER HEISENBERG (1901–1976) argued that one could not simultaneously know both the velocity and location of an element in the quantum world. In the subatomic realm, the act of observing an object by means of measurement disturbs the object of interest in ways that make it impossible to determine with precision the condition of the element.[19] Physicist Sir John Polkinghorne explains it in this way: "If you know where an electron is (position), you can't know what it's doing (momentum), and if you know what it's doing, you can't know where it is."[20]

Heisenberg suggested that quantum elements don't possess any definite characteristics that can be measured, only potentialities that become one thing or another during the process of measurement. Heisenberg posited the idea that we live in a reactive universe: "We can no longer speak of the behavior of the particle independently of the process of observation.... By its intervention science alters and refashions the object of investigation."[21]

Accordingly, attempts to measure quantum particles inexorably disturb them so that there can be no objective findings with regard to the momentum and position of particles. When particles are measured by high-frequency electromagnetic radiation, the energy of the measurement tools disturbs the movement of the particles in such a way that the original momentum can no longer be determined. Low-

---

19. Kaku and Thompson, *Beyond Einstein*, 43.
20. Polkinghorne, *Science and Theology*, 30.
21. Werner Heisenberg, *The Physicist's Conception of Nature*, trans. Arnold J. Pomerans (New York: Harcourt Brace, 1958), 15, 28–29.

frequency radiation does not disturb the momentum, but the long wavelengths make it impossible to determine position. We can measure one or the other, but not both.[22]

More recent findings indicate that such measurements can be taken. In a scientific report published in *Nature*, Niels Bohr Institute researchers—based on a number of experiments—demonstrated that Heisenberg's Uncertainty Principle can be neutralized to some degree. This has never been shown before, and the results may spark development of new measuring equipment as well as new and better sensors.[23]

> There is always some degree of uncertainty in the measurement. This is not inherent, or intrinsic uncertainty, but instead can be surpassed with the right application, for instance using the recent method developed by the research team at the Niels Bohr Institute.[24]

This is not as shocking as the finding that particles may react differently when they are not observed. It is only during measurement that "their ambiguous state of being is resolved into a definite position."[25] In quantum terms, measurement has consequences; it links the observer to the observed.

To translate this concept into cultural terms, one must consider the effect of measurement on human lives. There are no direct analogies between the phenomenon observed on quantum levels and social practices, but philosophical issues relevant to this discussion present themselves. Heisenberg said of the translation of scientific concepts into ordinary terms, "True, I often have great difficulty in grasping what these ideas are meant to convey, but when that happens, I always try to translate them into modern terminology and to discover whether they throw up

22. Tilby, *Soul*, 155–158.

23. Resonance Science Foundation Research Staff, "New Measurements Exceed Heisenberg Uncertainty Limit; Is This Experimental Evidence for Non-Orthodox Quantum Theories?" *Resonance Science Foundation*, n. d., https://resonance.is/new-measurements-exceed-heisenberg-uncertainty-limit-experimental-evidence-non-orthodox-quantum-theories/.

24. Ibid.

25. Tilby, *Soul*, 157.

fresh answers."[26] So I toss these ideas into the cultural maelstrom of intelligence testing.

We measure the progress of children through tests. Moreover, we require measurement to assess school achievement, corporate goals, and the effectiveness of teachers and administrators. What does it mean to say that measurement changes potential into stasis? An example may help to crystallize this illusive notion. When I was growing up, IQ tests were given in most schools and scores were shared with parents and children. The purported measurement of intelligence changed the lives of those who received the findings. Current tests that purport to measure achievement have a similar effect.

Of those who are measured, some are deemed intrinsically smart and capable of leadership, while others are no longer expected to achieve in publicly and socially preferred ways. Attorney and global activist Randall Robinson expresses it well: "We hardly ever in life exceed the expectations set for us by the general society. Some of us are conditioned to excel. Others are conditioned to fail. Few of us, however, are conditioned to give much conscious thought to where the bar has been set for us."[27]

Robinson refers to the gap between those who are expected to lead and achieve and those who are not as "some ageless yawning crevasse that separates the perennially privileged on their gilded higher ground from those who learn from birth to expect and therefore to reach for little."[28]

It is one thing to attribute such expectations, or the lack thereof, to innate ability, social circumstances, or fate; it is quite another to say that the universe, at its quantum levels, responds to the human desire to measure, record, and count by changing potential and possibilities into set options.

Perhaps God told David not to take a census, tally, or measurement of the people (see I Chronicles 21) because of the long-range effects and limited information that could be obtained. When we measure, we use tools that

26. Werner Heisenberg, "Truth Dwells in the Deeps," in *Quantum Questions: Mystical Writings of the World's Greatest Physicists*, ed. Ken Wilber (Boston: Shambhala, 2001), 36.

27. Randall Robinson, *The Debt: What America Owes to Blacks* (New York: Penguin, 2000), 62.

28. Ibid., 63.

fail to capture the spirit and tenor of human ability. In fact, standardized tests tend to measure only the ways in which we have assimilated the methodologies and empirical preferences of the dominant culture.

How does one measure potential? In quantum realms, one can ascertain position or momentum, but not both. For inner-city children, we may be able to ascertain where they are, but we will not be able to tell where or how far they are going. For dominant forces, uncertainty is uncomfortable and unsettling; for those struggling to gain a foothold in society, uncertainty offers the joy of open options.

Theologian and social psychologist Diarmuid O'Murchu offers another perspective as he describes the patriarchal urge in cosmic terms:

> Indeed, the patriarchal urge to dominate and control may be understood as an attempt to reduce the awesomeness of life to manageable proportions. . . . Our problem now is that we consider the primary reality to be that which has ensued from our reductionistic exploits. And this is beginning to prove deeply dissatisfying to the human spirit.[29]

In the quantum world there is a reality, but at the most fundamental levels it can only be described as potential. In our world there is potential in each and every human being; however, patriarchy, racism, and other oppressive systems limit and inhibit the options. We cannot take the measure of another human being with any accuracy. Tests only point to the place where potential might bloom.

Schrödinger's Cat

WORKING INDEPENDENTLY AND at the same time that Heisenberg was arriving at the uncertainty principle, Erwin Schrödinger (1887–1961) was proposing the potential of a dead/live cat. This experiment points to the fragility of reality. It seems that Schrödinger was inclined toward philosophical pursuits and Eastern religions prior to the publication of his equation.

29. O'Murchu, *Quantum Theology*, 29, 31.

In a note, he says, "This life of yours which you are living is not merely a piece of this entire existence, but is in a certain sense the 'whole'; only this whole is not so constituted that it can be surveyed in one single glance."[30]

Schrödinger also said, "I am in the east and in the west. I am below and above, I am this whole world."[31] In a discussion about this quote, physicist Fred Wolf argues that there are several realities that can be understood as "out there/in here." According to Wolf, it is a bridge of sorts between the worlds of the mind and the worlds of matter.[32]

Now to Schrödinger's thought puzzle. We are asked to consider an experiment that places a cat in a box or cage with a device containing a single quantum element. The observer cannot see into the box without lifting the lid. Michio Kaku suggests that we consider the element a single uranium nucleus. If the nucleus deteriorates and comes into contact with the triggering device, it will cause the release of poisonous gas.

But Schrödinger suggests that we cannot know the state of a single nucleus. Our calculations can only predict the state of many nuclei. So, we must rely on the formula that the nucleus has either deteriorated and killed the cat or is inert and the cat remains alive. In any event, before the box is opened, "the cat is statistically in the nether state of being dead *and* alive. If that isn't weird enough, the very act of opening the box decides whether the cat is dead or alive. According to quantum mechanics, the measurement process itself determines the state of the cat."[33]

The observer and the cat have no connection at the beginning of the experiment, but as the observer begins to contemplate the possibilities, a connection is formed. The observer is torn between two possibilities. As Wolf contends, "The universe has become two universes. In one, there is a living cat and a happy you, and in the other, there is a dead cat and a sad you."[34] Maybe, maybe not. Wolf refers to the state of mind of the observer before the box is opened and assumes a certain moral concern about the fate of the cat.

30. J. Bernstein, "I Am This Whole World: Erwin Schroedinger," in *Project Physics Reader 5* (New York: Holt, Reinhart and Winston, 1968–1969), 178, quoted in Wolf, *Taking the Quantum Leap*, 182.

31. Wolf, *Taking the Quantum Leap*, 182.

32. Ibid.

33. Kaku and Thompson, *Beyond Einstein*, 45.

34. Wolf, *Taking the Quantum Leap*, 190.

A new version of Schrödinger's cat has been offered by two scientists who call themselves "New Cats in Town." The authors, Daniela Frauchiger and Renato Renner of the Swiss Federal Institute of Technology (ETH) in Zurich, posted their first version of the argument online in April 2016. The final paper appeared in *Nature Communications* on September 18, 2018.[35] Although the details of their theory are beyond the scope of this discussion, their findings may mean that standard interpretations of quantum theory can give inconsistent descriptions of reality.

In cultural contexts, the "cats" in the box are often the poor and the oppressed. They often live in closed environments where there is the potential or actual release of deleterious elements (i.e., drugs, crime, economic impoverishment, and inferior educational systems). Like Schrödinger's cat, they are both dead and alive. One wonders if anyone is interested enough to lift the lid and find out.

To know the outcome of the puzzle, the observer must disturb the cage. This problem is reminiscent of the old puzzle, "If a tree falls in the forest, does it make noise if no one hears it?" It is a determination that cannot be made. The uncertainty principle makes the point that there are no neutral positions. In cultural contexts, when we assess one another and make deleterious or affirming assessments of worth and potential, we are affecting outcomes, but we are also being affected. If the essential elements of all matter are vibrating strings resonating at different frequencies, those resonances overlap.

In quantum terms, any choice that we make "is simply the collapse of the quantum wave function of possible thought into one definite thought."[36] Light is wave and particle; Schrödinger's cat is both dead and alive. In a multiverse, when choices and decisions are made here, the opposite choice or decision may be made in another parallel universe. In fact, quantum cosmologists posit the idea that measurements of quantum elements create a series of worlds. Each world has different possibilities and outcomes.[37] As bizarre as these theories may seem, they are

35. Daniela Frauchiger and Renato Renner, "Quantum Theory Cannot Consistently Describe the Use of Itself," *Nature Communications* 9, September 18, 2018, https://www.nature.com/articles/s41467-018-05739-8. Frauchiger has now left academia.

36. Zohar, *The Quantum Self*, 180.

37. Polkinghorne, *Science and Theology*, 29.

being taken seriously by physicists engaged in the pursuit of quantum knowledge.

Shattering Symmetries

QUANTUM COSMOLOGY PROPOSES that a universe can spring from a singularity or tiny point in the universe. Scientists assume that the big bang launched the expansion of our universe, which was symmetrical and without ascertainable features. The immediate description of the void in Genesis comes to mind but is not completely congruent with this model. As the universe cools, the symmetries break in the same way that water changes from a symmetrical fluidity to solid form with ice crystals.

> The universe, like the water in the glass, started off dense and homogenous. But as it expanded and cooled the symmetry was broken, not in a spatial sense, but in terms of its internal structure. So one force was distinguished from another, one particle type from another.[38]

The concept of symmetry can be beautiful and frightening. Physicist Michio Kaku tells the story of a princess stranded on a gigantic polished crystal ball. She lies atop the glistening orb in perfect symmetry, but, if she moves, she will fall to her death. Kaku says that her fall could be considered a period of transition that would break the symmetry; "thus the state of maximum symmetry is often an unstable state."[39]

Dominance and oppression create similar instabilities amid ostensible balance. For example, the exploitation of poor and indigenous communities creates a symmetry of sorts, as paltry wages flow into poverty-stricken areas of the world in exchange for child labor. In one video portrayal of a moral dilemma, two children, one from West Virginia and the other from India, toil at menial labor, one in a coal mine, another pasting thousands of paper cups together. Their hands bleed, their eyes are vacant, but the voice-over asks this question: "Would it be better for them to starve?"

---

38. Tilby, *Soul*, 168.
39. Kaku, *Hyperspace*, 211.

The question creates a conceptual symmetry, a quandary of survival and exploitation that matches the balanced flow of labor and low wages. It is a situation that can only be broken if the poor fall from the crystal sphere and refuse the funds that enslave and sustain them. Kaku refers to the potential for change as a "phase transition." In science, these transitions can be very violent, as in the explosion of an atomic bomb. The bomb explodes when neutrons bombard uranium nuclei or when, through radioactive decay, the nucleus splits without interference.

The transition from one phase to another in this case is explosive; the transition for besieged communities may erupt in a similar manner.

> The great Hebrew prophets presuppose a world full of big chances; they are on the lookout for contingencies—a world in which breaks in symmetry and the direction of time are possible. . . . In short, the universe must have a place in it not only for the laws of large numbers and immemorial tradition, but also a place in it for minorities of one or more that subvert a ruling order.[40]

Dominance requires symmetry between idolatrous self-esteem and static impoverishments of the spirit, control and disorder, hierarchy and collectivity. To break the yoke of dominance, these symmetries must be shattered, and the static properties of race relations must be altered. It is hoped that this phase transition will be as peaceful as the melting of ice into water, but there is always the potential for an explosion.[41]

Complementarity and the Human Possibility

THE LANGUAGE OF PHYSICS and cosmology invites cultural theorists to consider liberation within the context of unresolved dilemmas. "Instead of a simple 'either/or' structure, deconstruction attempts to elaborate a

40. Toolan, "Praying," 6.

41. See this update of a 2019 symmetry experiment: Physikalisch-Technische Bundesanstalt (PTB), "Testing the Symmetry of Space-Time by Means of Atomic Clocks: The Comparison of Two Atomic Clocks has Confirmed Their Excellent Accuracy as Well as a Fundamental Hypothesis of the Theory of Relativity," *Science Daily*, March 13, 2019, www.sciencedaily.com/releases/2019/03/190313143300.htm.

discourse that says *neither* 'either/or,' *nor* 'both/and' nor even 'neither/ nor,' while at the same time not totally abandoning these logics either."[42]

For example, complementarity engages the fundamental question, "Is light a wave or a particle?" The answer is that we can't pin down the essence of quantum or cultural elements. Instead, we are being encouraged to live with the tension of contradictory and opposing ideas. We are all good/evil, victims/victimizers. If the potential for the full spectrum of emotions and responses remained dynamic, abuse might end. It is the desire for certitude that allows us to veer toward one possibility or another.

Once the wave/particle potential collapses during our observations or measurements of one another, we take on a degraded aspect of humanity, for any manifestation of personhood that can be defined by one idea or another is idolatrous. The task before us is to return to a dynamic state and to allow others to do likewise.

We are challenged to not assign class, gender, sexuality, or cultural roles that limit and categorize. Instead, indeterminacy becomes the key factor in quantum realms. In the context of culture, an indeterminate realm unsettles our preset cultural categories. One state of being does not necessarily lead to a foregone conclusion. Poverty and race don't necessarily produce criminality.

For Jack Kevorkian (1928–2011), disability and severe health problems meant a life not worth living, but his opinion does not describe the outcome for Stephen Hawking and others who lived with both gifts and limitations. Perhaps indeterminacy is the foundation of free will. Since we can't predict the ultimate manifestation of human flourishing, all must be sustained and nurtured.

Summary

QUANTUM THEORIES PRESENT aspects of reality that overturn our previous assumptions. We really can't say what reality is or how it works. To date, we can say that the quantum world exists, but its contours are elusive and potential rather than actual. With all this potential emerging,

---

42. Barbara Johnson, *A World of Difference* (Baltimore: Johns Hopkins University Press, 1987), 12.

something is missing. It is the potential of the two-thirds world. Yet, even with its exclusion, dominance and victimization are only one aspect of reality, an aspect that is not insurmountable.

The possibility of mutuality still beckons us, because no person or society can fill the categories of victimizer or oppressor permanently and totally. We are creatures of potential and possibility, embodying many aspects of reality simultaneously.

seven

Everything is enfolded in everything.

—David Bohm,
Wholeness and the Implicate Order

::::

There is a danger in forgetting what you must remember.
There is a danger in remembering what you must forget.
There is a danger in staying when you must depart in faith.

—Walter F. Brueggemann,
Threat of Life:
Sermons on Pain, Power, and Weakness

::::

⁜ 7 ⁜

A Community-Called-Beloved

> I concluded that community is that place where the person you least want to live with always lives. . . . When that person moves away, someone else arises immediately to take his or her place! So I think part of being in community is always having to face ourselves in the mirror of another, frequently our nemesis.
>
> —Parker Palmer, "Spiritual Formation and Change"

PALMER IS CORRECT. Community, beloved or not, is a place of human contradictions. It is where we desire to be, but it is also the site of interaction with those who provoke, inspire, and challenge our efforts to be relational. Yet, we continue to seek this idyllic space. Like others, I wondered why the notion of the beloved community persists into the twenty-first century, when other optimistic concepts and metaphors taken from the Civil Rights movement have fallen into disuse.

I believe we continue to muse about the possibility because of the beauty of the concepts and analogies that emerged from the prophetic speech of Martin Luther King, Jr. He described the beloved community as a reconciling and safe place where people of all nations could enter with the innocence of children and dwell in this place of peace. The phrase "beloved community" was coined by American philosopher Josiah Royce (1855–1916), but it was King's sermonic descriptions of the beloved community that became an anthem of intent, a melody of purpose. King offered a divided nation "the substance of things hoped for, the evidence of things unseen" (Hebrews 11:1).

In this chapter, I am considering whether the idea of a community-called-beloved, a reconciled collective of caring people, can arise from the ashes of hope unborn. If this dream is also an attainable goal, how do we get there from here? If the community-called-beloved is nothing more than a rhetorical device used to consider the mutuality of a guilt-ridden, conflicted, and racially ambivalent nation, then the two-thirds world needs to find another symbol of their liberation.

Either the beloved community was a dream for simpler times, or we need to expand the concept beyond social, religious, and theological limits to include a wider cosmological context.

Can We Dream Together?

FORTUNATELY—OR NOT—dreaming is a solitary endeavor. As Alfred Schütz notes, "We cannot dream together."[1] When we are dreaming, there is a complete relaxation of the attention to life. Dreaming is, in essence, a complete turning away. Although, as Sigmund Freud (1856–1939) argued, dreams may be filled with volition, purpose, and even unconscious impulses that don't surface during the waking state, dreaming is not a social endeavor.

However, we can share visions, which are the collective expressions of individual dreams, revelations, and insights. From a phenomenological standpoint, dreams may inspire and even inform us, but we can't build communities on dreams. Even if we could, they would remain just beyond our reach, as there are no road maps to utopia. However, Anthony Cook does not believe that King's dream was completely utopian.

---

1. Alfred Schütz and Thomas Luckmann, *The Structures of the Life-World*, trans. Richard M. Zaner and H. Tristram Engelhardt, Jr. (Evanston, IL: Northwestern University Press, 1973), 34.

King's vision of a Beloved Community flowed out of his synthesis of pragmatic, individualist-centered and spiritually oriented understandings of the African-American religious tradition with the prophetic, community-centered and socially oriented dimensions of the same tradition.[2]

Martin Luther King, Jr. had a dream, but he was not alone. Many visions of equality and justice merged during his famous speech. Upon hearing it, an entire nation was convinced that an egalitarian society was possible. For the first time since the birth of the nation, racially divided segments of the society shared this vision of mutuality.

It never occurred to us that several decades later we would be wide awake, ethically numb, and more acquainted with nightmares than dreams. Yet the warning signs were all there. Those who slay dragons in their sleep will wake up with rumpled beds and little else. It is not that King failed us; he brought the vision to our attention as a good prophet should and then began to demonstrate the avenues of possible fulfillment.

We were expecting a straight path to unity; instead, like the chaotic movements of subatomic particles, many options erupted out of nowhere. According to King, the beloved community presupposed empowerment of the poor, the cessation of wars, a more egalitarian economy, and an end to polite deceptions about systematic abuse.

On behalf of these goals, he spoke out about the war in Vietnam, planned the Poor People's March on Washington, and spoke truth to power about the global economic machine that was grinding people to powder. When a bullet finally silenced him, we mourned but also relaxed, nodding off to a less intense version of the dream. This beloved community that we envisioned in the aftermath of the assassination differed from King's vision, as it was primarily rhetorical and utopian. But, most importantly, it did not require our muscle, resolve, or risk. During slavery, those who dreamed and ran for freedom paid a high price.

Theologian and ethicist Riggins Earl discusses earlier cultural interpretations of dreams as a message matrix for social and theological

---

2. Cook, *The Least of These*, 135.

enlightenment within the context of slave conversion.[3] Individual dreams and shared visions offered besieged people a location for freedom of thought.

Such was the case in the pre-civil rights African American community. Foreclosed from meaningful interaction in the national community, African Americans shared the vision of a time when the playing field would be level. During this time, the black church was not just a faith community, but was also a locus of social power. In the worst of times, houses of prayer and brush arbors offered a modicum of protection from dangerous public spaces. It was in those safe spaces and worship times that the potential for a beloved community began to crystallize into a landscape.

According to Anthony E. Cook, King's beloved community had specific spiritual, social, and strategic contours. The spiritual aspects addressed the dire state of African American interiority and the need for a "psychospiritual conversion . . . which would then serve as the catalyst for social conversion."[4] The social strata of the community would use justice and love as "normative guidance for critical intelligence and democratic process,"[5] and the strategic dimension would be a modality for synthesizing integrationist and nationalistic perspectives. The process became as important as the goal.

Talk about the beloved community changed the national consciousness. It is not just a matter of timing that determines which discourse will shift the ideology of a nation. For years before the Civil Rights movement, spokespersons like Ida B. Wells-Barnett (1862–1931) decried the lynching and systematic abuse of the African American community. Her pleas for the most part fell on deaf ears.

The nation would not peer into the mirror that she held up, for, in her appeal, society heard accusations that challenged long-standing civic mantras of equality and goodness. In contrast, images of the "beloved community" did not challenge civic mythologies, but offered a liturgy of hope and potential as well as the unlikely alliances of friends and foes.

---

3. Riggins R. Earl, Jr., *Dark Symbols, Obscure Signs: God, Self, and Community in the Slave Mind* (Maryknoll, NY: Orbis, 1993).

4. Cook, *The Least of These*, 135.

5. Ibid., 136.

However, I am concerned that civic and theological images of the community-called-beloved have become confused and conflated into models of reconciliation that bear no resemblance to our prior expectations. Civic religion in North America describes the beloved community as a gathering of healed, whole, and loving people who aspire to the highest good for all. But it also encodes assumptions about global supremacy and "an arrogant defense of our present way of life."[6]

This is not the description of community derived from Holy Scripture. The Judeo-Christian version of God's reconciled community is one where all the inhabitants are broken and oppressed by sin. Joseph Barndt contends that everyone is in need of liberation and redemption. He says that "the last thing popular American religion will accept is the idea that white, middle-class Americans are oppressed or enslaved, either by racism or by any other power."[7] The label "middle-class" also entices POC to view themselves in similar ways. However, if the universe is as holistic and interconnected as we now suppose, then all of us are enslaved and oppressed by hatred and by our myopic identification of enemies.

Beloved Enemies

WHEN DID THE PARADOX of love and hate, good and evil collapse into the clear identification of enemies? I can understand the political manipulations of language to identify "evil ones" who will be the targets of military aggression, but, in cultural contexts, how can we look in a mirror and still be certain about the face of the enemy? Is the exclusion of difference the premise upon which the community-called-beloved can be built?

Membership in a community is based as much on exclusion of the "unlike" as it is on inclusion. In a situation of oppression, considering one's community to be chosen can be a valuable support; in a

6. Joseph Barndt, *Dismantling Racism: The Continuing Challenge to White America* (Minneapolis: Augsburg, 1991, 2009), 46. See also Barbara Trepagnier, *Silent Racism: How Well-Meaning White People Perpetuate the Racial Divide*, 2nd ed. (New York: Routledge, 2016).

7. Ibid.

situation of dominance it can be dangerous. Actually, the view can be dangerous even when held by the oppressed; the Israelites were not a powerful people when they believed themselves called to eliminate the Canaanites.[8]

It has taken a while to realize that we derive significant gains from the presence of enemies. According to theologian David Barash, "At the level of adult society, interaction, even hostile interaction, often yields stability, so long as the patterns are crisscrossing and do not tend repeatedly to fracture at the same places."[9] However, for conflict to be efficacious, it must be specific and defined. We can disagree about some things, but not all things. If we draw battle lines as to race and justice, we must still have issues of consensus in work, worship, or participation in the market economy.

We are talking about constantly shifting alliances. "It may seem paradoxical, but society can thus be sewn together by its inner conflicts. Enemies and allies are the warp and woof of our social fabric, as the shuttle spins and flashes through the diverse and shifting connections of modern life."[10] Examples of the phenomenon abound. We deplore crime and are galvanized into communities by our sense of righteous indignation and the desire to provide protection against criminal assault. Political rivalries and scandal evoke discomfort but focus the collective political consciousness on the task of government.

When enemies are apparent, we present a united front. Although unity is the primary benefit, it is usually a temporary and fragile benefit that cannot sustain a healthy community. Our battle readiness also takes a toll, leaving us with a sense of overwhelming confusion. One theorist describes the feeling in this way: "I felt both too powerful and not powerful enough at the same time, like a rebel who woke up to find himself emperor of a realm he

---

8. Elizabeth M. Bounds, "Conflicting Harmonies: Michael Walzer's Vision of Community," *Journal of Religious Ethics* 22, no. 2 (Fall 1994): 368. See also Jim Ife, *Community Development in an Uncertain World: Vision, Analysis, and Practice* (New York: Cambridge University Press, 2013).

9. David P. Barash, *Beloved Enemies: Our Need for Opponents* (Amherst, NY: Prometheus, 1994), 131. See also David P. Barash, *Through a Glass Brightly: Using Science to See Our Species as We Really Are* (New York: Oxford University Press, 2018).

10. Ibid.

had spent his life trying to destroy."[11] Fighting the good fight takes energy, bravery, and a critical acceptance of struggle as a way of life.

Because the act of defining and labeling enemies is so subjective, wise designees will turn the tables at the most unlikely times. Philosopher Michael Barber notes that

> an in-group interprets the out-group, but the in-group also interprets the out-group's interpretation of the in-group. This...looking glass affect between races [sic]...manifests an in-group so intent upon preserving its status that it anticipates objections from the out-group, and attributes those objections to the out-group's defensiveness, thereby immunizing itself against any possibility of critique from the out-group.[12]

Barber has described a situation that would defy even the most serious attempt to reconcile a national community, but the *basileia* of God is just as problematic. Eden contains snakes and temptations, as well as a disobedient and deceptive couple. As it turns out, the community-called-beloved has its discomforts and foibles. Community is not just a love fest; it is also a site of dialectical tension.

We peer into mirrors that bear our own reflection. When asked, the sage in the mirror may tell us that we are the future of the world, a multicultural and beloved community. Is it true, or are we deluded by our own presuppositions? How will we know if we can't find words to describe the community that we so earnestly seek?

Words of Power

THEOLOGIAN EDWARD FARLEY described words of power as deep and enduring symbols that help to shape our vision of society and our relationships with one another. Farley wrote that words of power are

---

11. Robert Inchausti, *Spitwad Sutras: Classroom Teaching as Sublime Vocation* (Westport, CT: Bergin & Garvey, 1993), 167.

12. Michael Barber, "The Ethics Behind the Absence of Ethics in Alfred Schütz's Thought," *Human Studies: A Journal for Philosophy and the Social Sciences* (July 1991): 129–140.

imperatives that "arise within and express the historical determinacy of a community."[13] He went on to say that "deep symbols have at least the following four features: normativity, enchantment, fallibility (relativity and corruptibility) and location in a master narrative."[14]

These commands carry meaning and power and are primarily depicted as positive and transcendent signals, covenants, and values. Yet there are reasons to believe that Farley's words of power have opposite imperatives that emerge out of negative or destructive energies addressed by the "thou shalt nots."

These shadow symbols influence, skew, and shape our consciousness in the same way as their positive twins. There is precedent for this assumption in the new cosmology. Cosmologists have determined that our universe is full of unseen dimensions and objects. We measure and "see" the galaxies and their components by emitted light. Those objects that dwell in the shadow must be measured by other means, or their existence is inferred by the impact that they have on other objects. Dark matter is such a substance.

Dark matter can be concisely described as the unseen glue of the universe that holds together rapidly spinning galaxies. It controls the rate at which the universe expands and its future. Yet, to date, we can detect its presence only because of the gravitational pull on other systems. Scientists Marc David, Richard Muller, and Piet Hut also discuss shadow realms and substances. They have suggested that our sun may have had a shadow sun, an unseen twin they have named "nemesis."[15] Today, it is commonly believed that stars/suns are born in litters and that our sun is no exception.[16]

I am suggesting that words of power (deep symbols) have parallel words of power (shadow symbols), unseen opposites that can be detected only by the effects they have on our utopian agendas. The discourses of racism constitute a powerful shadow discourse. Farley attributed the loss

---

13. Farley, *Deep Symbols*, 3.

14. Ibid.

15. Michael S. Turner, "The Universe," *Science Year* (1994): 195; quoted in Crosley, *The Vodou Quantum Leap*, 78.

16. Robert Sanders, "New Evidence that All Stars Are Born in Pairs," *Berkeley News*, June 13, 2017, https://news.berkeley.edu/2017/06/13/new-evidence-that-all-stars-are-born-in-pairs/.

of positive words of power with alienation from communities of human intimacy.[17] I am suggesting that some of the losses can be attributed to shadow words of power, which include racism and xenophobia, that are affecting the relevance, primacy, and effectiveness of Farley's positive discursive formulation.

Positive words of power have a "normative character" because "they summon the community out of its corrupted present."[18] Although Farley acknowledged negative opposites, the "thou shall nots," they are depicted as the opposite of the vision for betterment and as inclinations that can be overcome. My suggestion is that shadow words of power are normative to the extent that they embody and project the unexpressed but deeply historical responses to difference that have become normative in dominant cultures. While expressions of summoning to betterment prevail, actions that express the continuing and powerful hatred of difference continue to beset us.

The discussion of enchantment relates words of power to faith-based origins. "Enchantment means the way finite reality participates in sacred power."[19] These words have a history tied to mystery and the ineffable realities of Holy Scripture and discernment. Yet shadow words of power are everywhere in the media and in our sermons. The shadow opposite of enchantment is radical individualism and autonomy.

Finally, words of power are also associated with a master narrative. One of postmodernity's gifts was the shattering of master narratives to expose the stories and specific geo-cultural locations of silenced people, including LGBTQIA+, women, and inhabitants of the two-thirds world. Because master narratives have played a role in the suppression and violation of human rights, I am suspicious of them. I am also reluctant to embrace grand narratives that synthesize and summarize, because the languages of the new physics tell us that the universe is chaotic and increasingly unpredictable. Although we presume an underlying order, we can't fit what we are learning into any verifiable formula.

The question that should be asked about master narratives is whether African Americans and other marginalized communities are reshaping and participating in the master's/master narrative or whether they have

17. Farley, *Deep Symbols*, x.
18. Ibid., 4.
19. Ibid., 5.

a narrative of their own that may be symbiotic but also conflictual and shadowy. To explicate these shadowy discourses, I return to the example of the O. J. Simpson trial as a tale of two deeply felt, deeply believed, and very historical and powerful narratives. The African American narratives and shadowy words of power did not collide with dominant assumptions until the verdict was rendered.

The news media called it a tale of two Americas (leaving out Native American, Hispanic, Asian, and other interests), but it may have been the emergence of a shadow discourse as powerful and as transcendent as the "normative" view. The healthy turn toward self-understanding is communal rather than narcissistic. Knowing implies a responsibility to the larger social collective, but responsibility is not just a local or global concept. It is also cosmic. Cosmologists are now aware that if the ratio of one element to another were different, life could not be sustained on this planet. How can we shirk our responsibilities to one another when the universe provides such a balanced system of care for us? Even if one considers this "care" in the most scientific sense, it only makes sense that, as constituent human parts of this interrelated and sustaining whole, we are called to act in a similar manner.

The community-called-beloved is not a static idea; it can be revised. During the 1960s, we imagined such a community through the image of children of different ethnic backgrounds playing together. Perhaps we need a different vision as we enter the year 2020, a vision that includes mutual obligations and belonging. Obligation is the awareness of our intrinsic connectedness to one another. This is Farley's proposition: "If there is to be any obligation at all, there must be transcendent others in the world that do not mirror or duplicate the self: others, whose life orientations, aims, needs, and agendas do not coincide with our own."[20]

The choice is ours: We can use strangers to demarcate lines of separation, or we can seek the growing edges toward which difference prods us. Unfortunately, litigious Western societies often allow the interhuman aspects of obligation and responsibility to be co-opted by legal interpretations. These interpretations can divorce duty from "the vulnerable face of the other" and skew benefits toward privileged sectors of society.[21]

20. Ibid., 48.

21. Ibid., 52–54. Farley acknowledged the difficulty of subsuming the full content of

Farley proposed that the concept of obligation can be "re-embodied" if we situate it in communal, face-to-face contexts. Doing so reconnects us to the participatory holism of the universe. Our senses tell us that we are solitary beings traversing a placid life space. Scientists offer another view. They contend that we are connected to others through energy, resonance, and perhaps shared consciousness.

Essentially, we are beings of energy and light in a universe that emits both. Recently, biophysicists have identified energy in the form of photon radiation, which is present in living cells and may regulate their coherent operation.[22] As strange as it may seem, living entities (including human beings) can produce light within their bodies and brains that can be detected outside of the body.

We are being bombarded by unseen elements that carry energy, and we are generating it from within our own bodies. In this interdependent and dynamic cosmos, there should be enough "energy" to focus on issues of diversity and reconciliation.

We have always seen social disorder and conflict as problems limited to the public sphere. However, science is revealing that our antagonisms have physical as well as social consequences. "People who are in conflict—and this is most of us to some degree—have much less energy available to the main personality (their highest unity) than people who are more integrated."[23] It seems that the struggles for and against justice may unsettle our biological balances.

Moreover, the new physics speaks of connections that are not limited to the social world but are intrinsic elements of the universe. When we try to distance ourselves from this reality, we reap distortions of guilt and alienation. Even more sobering is the thought that the universe encodes within its unspoken mandates prophetic elements that hint at our demise if we refuse the mantle of self- and communal governance. By governance,

the word "obligation" in juridical notions, since the ritualized jousting that emanates from the law constrains the potential of the term.

22. Fritz-Albert Popp et al., "Physical Aspects of Biophotons," *Experientia* 44 (1988), 576–585. See also Lucas W. E. Tessaro, Blake T. Dotta, and Michael A. Persinger, "Bacterial Biophotons as Non-Local Information Carriers: Species-Specific Spectral Characteristics of a Stress Response," *MicrobiologyOpen*, October 31, 2018, https://onlinelibrary.wiley.com/doi/10.1002/mbo3.761; and Zohar, *The Quantum Self*, 85.

23. Zohar, *The Quantum Self*, 116.

I refer to the necessity of defining and nurturing the common good, not just for humankind, but also for the earth and its varied life forms. Responsibility and obligation are not merely ethical paradigms and philosophical constructs; they are also learned behaviors and actual states of becoming and fulfillment.

If we truly want to be responsible, we must first be aware that the process of "growing up" in Western cultures includes learning to accomplish along the lines that society affirms. Despite these cultural habituations, we can revise our suppositions about the life journey. Sometimes it takes a sweaty metaphysical wrestling match with malaise, nihilism, self-absorption, and egoism to reach the desired balance of belonging, altruism, and responsibility.

A Scientific Reclamation of Wholeness and Community

ANY COMMUNITY that we construct on earth will be only a small model of a universe whose community includes billions of stars and planetary systems. Are we alone? We don't know, but if we don't know how to become a community with our own species, how shall we find harmony with other life forms in the cosmos? Our ideas of community begin with fragmentation, difference, and disparity seeking wholeness.

Our beloved community is an attempt to hot-glue disparate cultures, language, and ethnic origins into one mutually committed whole. The universe tells a completely different story—that everything is enfolded into everything.[24]

Physicist David Bohm urged a reconsidering of our commitments to fragmentation. Even though the languages of the new physics and cosmology discard mechanistic understandings of the universe in favor of potential, we love order. We see it where it doesn't exist and impose it through our narratives. Everything that we do conceals the unity that seems to be intrinsic to our life space. We take pictures of objects that seem to be outside of self, we demarcate national boundaries, we align

24. David Bohm, *Wholeness and the Implicate Order* (New York: Routledge, 1996), 177.

with friends and break with enemies, we give and receive in what seem to be neat sequential packets of life and experience.

By contrast, Bohm described the universe as a whole or implicate order that is "our primary reality . . . the subtle and universal reservoir of all life, the wellspring of all possibility, and the source of all meaning."[25] The life space, Bohm wrote, is the explicate order that unfolds as a visible and discernible aspect of this unseen wholeness. As Diarmuid O'Murchu notes, "What we perceive, therefore, is not a landscape of facts or objects, but one of events, of processes, movement, and energy. In this creative flow, past, present, and future are indistinguishable."[26]

The notion is intriguing and strange. Somehow concepts of time merge and recede into a continuum of energy and possibility. The concept got even more captivating when Bohm wrote that the universe is a hologram. To understand what he meant, one must understand the science of holography. The mathematician Dennis Gabor (1900–1979) introduced the idea in 1947.[27] A hologram is a dimensional projection of an object that encodes the whole image in its parts. For example, the projection of some part of the body enlarged may project the whole person.

Perhaps in ways that we don't yet understand, the struggle for justice on many fronts is an enfolding image of the whole—the embodiment of a holistic and unfragmented community. This community, viewed from a holographic perspective, would not be the logical outcome of progressive movements toward an ascertainable external goal, but would be the sum of past, present, and future expectations and disappointments. Then the community-called-beloved becomes all that we can and cannot conceive, all that lies beyond the horizon of apprehension but is available to us as part of the matrix of wholeness.

This description seems particularly esoteric because the desire for concrete goals and accomplishments lingers. However, if we are not bound by the myth of inexorable progress, we won't be discouraged when events seem to enfold into one another in ways that are not attentive to the concepts of past/present/future. Thanks to Einstein, we know that time is relative and progress is perspectival. Given this scenario, we don't

25. O'Murchu, *Quantum Theology*, 62; see also Bohm's discussion, Ibid., 172–196.
26. Ibid., 58.
27. Ibid., 55.

have to wait for the event of liberation to dawn. Moreover, our initiatives toward justice and reconciliation are no longer Herculean leaps of faith or miraculous feats of social engineering.

We are one, and our wars and racial divisions cannot defeat the wholeness that lies just below the horizon of human awareness. But there are other scientific affirmations of human connections. The diversity for which we strive in the community-called-beloved may be the matrix of the universe.

> If the universe really is structured to organize itself spontaneously through time, drinking energy from its environment and bursting out in new and novel creations, we should perhaps be less mono-lithic and idealistic in our view of what faith might draw from us. God not only seems to tolerate diversity, but to require it.[28]

Diversity may not be a function of human effort or justice. It may just be the sea in which we swim. To enact a just order in human communities is to reclaim a sense of unity with divine and cosmological aspects of the life space. As Hebrew Scripture scholar Terence Fretheim suggests, the "Let us" discourse in Genesis is a statement of the community of God.

God is creating and ordering the universe, but does not do it alone. Because the rhetoric is pluralistic, the reasonable assumption is that God is in relationship not only with humankind, but also with a divine community. Some Christians explain this divine collectivity in terms of the Trinity. Others ponder the sources of relationality that emerge from scientific realms.

Bell's Theorem of Interconnectedness

IF WE ARE going to consider community from a scientific perspective, we cannot neglect theories of non-locality or the interconnectedness of quantum elements. Albert Einstein disliked intensely the random aspect of quantum theory and the presumption that observers may affect out-

---

28. Tilby, *Soul*, 202.

comes. He said, "I can't imagine that a mouse could drastically change the universe by merely looking at it."[29]

In an effort to emphasize the incompleteness of quantum theory, Einstein and his colleagues Boris Podolsky (1896–1966) and Nathan Rosen (1909–1995) devised an experiment in 1935 that used two "momentum-correlated electrons." Bell used a simpler version in the form of "two polarization-correlated photons."[30] Both experiments came to the same verifiable conclusion.[31]

When two particles that have been paired travel in opposite directions, measurements indicate a correlation of characteristics that are indicative of the pair rather than a single element. This occurs even though there has been no direct contact between the two. The distances are so great that no force or energy could cause the effect. The experiment brings us to the conclusion that we are connected. "At a deep and fundamental level, the 'separate parts' of the universe are connected in an intimate and immediate way."[32] The best way to describe this phenomenon of quantum theory is simply to state the incredible. "Once two quantum entities have interacted with each other, they retain a power to influence each other, no matter how widely they subsequently might separate."[33]

Scientists don't know how this occurs. If it is a matter of communication between the particles, then those impulses and informational transfers are superluminal or occurring faster than the speed of light. Our current scientific knowledge does not allow for such speeds. For years, physicists were stumped. Then John Bell (1928–1990), an Irish theoretical physicist, began to explore the issue of quantum reality. His theories suggested that "reality" in quantum events is non-local. This means that

29. Quoted without attribution in Herbert, *Quantum Reality*, 200–201.

30. Ibid., 201.

31. In recent years, the research supports "spooky action" at a distance. Adrian Cho, "More Evidence to Support Quantum Theory's 'Spooky Action at a Distance,'" *Science*, August 28, 2015, https://www.sciencemag.org/news/2015/08/more-evidence-support-quantum-theory-s-spooky-action-distance.

32. Zukav, *Dancing Wu Li*, 282. See also Elizabeth Fernandez, "Can Reality Ever Be Known? A Tribute to Bell's Theorem," *Forbes*, July 2, 2019, https://www.forbes.com/sites/fernandezelizabeth/2019/07/02/can-reality-ever-be-known-a-tribute-to-bells-theorem/#4d5f8ea23869.

33. Polkinghorne, *Science and Theology*, 31.

particles or elements separated by vast distances react as if they are still connected.

The measurement of one element affects the other even though they are no longer in direct contact. Bell's findings are based on the Einstein-Podolsky-Rosen paradox. Physicist Nick Herbert offers a succinct summary of non-local influences. His way of describing these unusual effects is to say that "non-local interaction is . . . *unmediated, unmitigated,* and *immediate.*"[34] His conclusion alerts us to connections that are instantaneous over great distances. These cannot be seen but speak of relationality that is informative for our discussion of community.

For those of us who have been in connection because our histories have intertwined, disconnection may not be an option. Moreover, our influences on the flourishing and well-being of others may not require direct contact. There are certainly cultural examples of non-locality. The most obvious is the assertion of vodou practitioners that harm can be inflicted from a distance. Experts in human mental processes make similar assertions that thinking may not be located in the physical processes of the brain.

Even more interesting is the idea that our desires for community may not have a completely theological or social origin, but may, instead, be a reflection of our own physical and quantum connections to a relational cosmos. Theologian O'Murchu puts it well when he says that "the search for community is not merely a pursuit of security and intimacy to obviate our loneliness in an anonymous and impersonal world. It is much more than that. It is the expression . . . of a yearning from deep within the created order itself."[35] He continues, citing Brian Swimme and Thomas Berry, "Our broken, fragmented world yearns to be whole again. We humans imbibe this longing and, on behalf of creation, we give it conscious expression, particularly in our desire and efforts to re-create a sense of the earthly and cosmic community."[36]

34. Herbert, *Quantum Reality*, 214. See also George S. Greenstein, *Quantum Strangeness: Wrestling with Bell's Theorem and the Ultimate Nature of Reality* (Cambridge, MA: MIT Press, 2019).

35. O'Murchu, *Quantum Theology*, 89.

36. Ibid., citing Brian Swimme and Thomas Berry, *The Universe Story* (San Francisco: HarperSanFrancisco, 1992), 257.

It is encouraging to think that our missteps and failures in the effort to create community are not the final story. However, we are limited by our senses and cannot view or understand a holistic cosmos. That which seems empty is full; that which seems disconnected is linked. As physicist David Bohm suggested, everything is enfolded into everything at the same time that holographic projections of the whole are unfolding from fragmentary pieces.

Ultimately, the universe will not sanction our divisions; instead, the cosmos groans for the restorative acts of humankind. But, before we can bring the community to fruition, we must have a clearer vision of the community-called-beloved.

Beloved Apparitions

THE MOVIE *Beloved*, based on the novel of the same name written by Pulitzer Prize-winning novelist Toni Morrison (1931–2019), met with mixed reviews despite the supportive star power of Oprah Winfrey. Some audiences recoiled from a story of slavery that seemed to have no happy ending.

A runaway enslaved woman named Sethe kills a child and intends to kill the others to keep them from returning to slavery. The dead child, who becomes a woman in the spirit world, is called "Beloved." She haunts and seduces the main characters throughout the remainder of the film until the women of the community come together in a collective act of exorcism to reclaim the family. The child "Beloved" seems to be a symbol of the haunting legacies that slavery bequeathed. In an interview with Charlie Rose, Morrison said, "The question in this novel was, 'Who is the beloved?'"[37]

The question that Morrison posed, among others, needs to be considered in a cultural context. Can we identify the beloved in the community for which we yearn? What elements are beloved, and why are we haunted

---

37. Toni Morrison, "Interview with Charlie Rose," *The Charlie Rose Show*, Public Broadcasting System, January 19, 1998. See also Toni Morrison, "No Place for Self-Pity, No Room for Fear," *The Nation*, March 23, 2015, https://www.thenation.com/article/no-place-self-pity-no-room-fear/.

by the vision? What can be restored and reclaimed, and what must be mourned? How are we to exorcise the demonic presences of past offenses and conflicts?

Perhaps public theology offers the best option to rid our hopes of these invasive spiritual weights. Public theology can move difficult discussions into multicultural and interfaith spheres. The contributions of a conflicted society can help to realign our mantras of reconciliation with the pragmatic opportunities available to this generation.

Summary

IF THE BELOVED COMMUNITY is a dream, it is situated in quantum realms that evince potential as a past, present, and future reality accessible to us in a multidimensional universe. Einstein taught us that time is relative and the future and past are malleable concepts. If we give up the progressive and linear view of "progress," we may begin to approach the community-called-beloved.

Having reached the limits of protest, and after decades of struggle, activists paused to reflect, mourn, and seek personal fulfillment. It is time again to assess the future of a reconciled community and to develop new rhetorical options to describe and sustain our vision. Perhaps the community-called-beloved is the universe in all its expanding, relational, and quixotic beauty. Physicist Bohm believed that the universe is in conversation with us as it expands. To accept this premise means that nothing is as it seems. Our lives may be manifesting as a dialogue between creation, created, and Creator.

The community-called-beloved is personal, theological, and scientific. It is here and not here, for there is no here or there. We breathe and excrete and sing the beloved community; we discuss and imprison it. Sometimes we give it a lethal injection concocted from the pomposity and determination that we are right about the ways of the world. Even then it does not die—Thanks be to God.

eight

To inquire after the meaning or object of one's own existence
or of creation generally has always seemed to me absurd
from an objective point of view. . . .
In this sense, I have never looked upon ease and happiness
as ends in themselves—
such an ethical basis I call more proper for a herd of swine.
The ideals which have lighted me on my way
and time after time given me new courage to face life cheerfully,
have been Truth, Goodness, and Beauty.

—Albert Einstein,
The World as I See It

⁞⁞⁞

"More connects us than separates us.
But in times of crisis the wise build bridges,
while the foolish build barriers.
We must find a way to look after one another
as if we were one single tribe."

—King T'Challa,
in *Black Panther*

⁞⁞⁞

::: *8* :::

The Search for Meaning

*I say meaning is being! So any transformation of society
must result in a profound change of meaning.*
—David Bohm

The world is so silent about significance.
—Albert Camus

O N   T H E   C A M P U S of the Oblate School of Theology in San Anto-
nio, Texas, there is a grotto and replicas of our Lady of Lourdes
and the Virgin of Guadalupe. On a warm summer night, candles
flickered in the dark as the faithful gathered to pray. I was returning from
an evening session of a faculty workshop at the Hispanic Summer Program when some of the participants stopped to gaze at the lit statue of
the Virgin Mary. Candles glittered at her feet as supplicants knelt. It took
a moment to realize that a large white dove sat on Mary's head. At first,
it seemed that the bird was a part of the alabaster sculpture. Its cooing
alerted us to the fact that it was real. We watched the motionless dove for
what seemed like a long time.

As we walked away, I mentioned that the scene was rich with meaning.
Here was a symbol of the Holy Spirit perched on Mary's head. Another

member of the group reminded me that it probably meant that doves like sheltered coves. Other meanings surfaced and faded until we were silent again, listening to the utterances of the faithful and the dove.

The search for meaning is an intrinsic part of human life. We search for it in the most incongruous places. When it eludes our grasp, we spin webs of delicious deception, perform acts of mimetic creation, and project our limited perspectives on the whole. For fleeting moments, when things are going our way or when insight pierces the taken-for-granted everyday world, we proclaim to all who will listen that we have found "meaning." We want the "good life" and we want to be "happy," but what does that mean in a cosmic perspective?

For Einstein, ease and happiness were not ends in themselves. To the contrary, he deemed such pursuits and ethical predicates appropriate for a herd of swine, but not for humankind. This is a harsh assessment, to be certain, but one that jolts the imagination. Should we avoid the pigsty that Einstein conjures or wallow and enjoy the brief life segments that we are given? Why are we here and what is the meaning of the human journey? As Diarmuid O'Murchu notes, "The drive toward meaning comes from deep within—not just within ourselves, but also . . . from deep within creation itself."[1]

One could arrive at this conclusion after surveying the recent findings of physicists and cosmologists that the universe is responsive. The inference is that design and consciousness may point to an initiating divinity and a responsive universe. Of course, we want to know the length and breadth of this responsiveness; however, each mystery points to another. Despite wondrous advances, we are no closer to the "truth" of the cosmic plan today than we were when humans first observed the wonder of an isolated atom or night sky. However, there are fascinating scientific speculations that can inform our cultural tasks.

1. O'Murchu, *Quantum Theology*, 12.

Design or Accident:
The Anthropic Principle

ONE THING IS CERTAIN. If we are to glean meaning, the context must include the overall picture of the universe and our place in it. The anthropic principle considers the unique cosmic events and balance of galactic forces that had to occur in the right proportions to sustain life. Scientists refer to the theory in the singular, even though there are weak and strong versions. The strong anthropic principle says that the universe requires observers.

This hypothesis is subdivided into three ideas. First, the universe is unique and has come into existence with the "intent" of sustaining conscious observers. Second, many universes exist, and life is inevitable in such an immense cosmos. Third, the universe could only come into being if there were conscious observers.[2] In the words of physicist Freeman Dyson, "The universe knew we were coming."[3]

The ideas became even more estranged from common knowledge in the work of scientist John Wheeler (1911–2008), who contended that quantum principles make it possible for observers in the future to affect the past within the framework of a universe that he described as "a self-excited circuit."[4] According to this theory, reality emerges from the reflexive act of human engagement with the past. This statement requires more of an explanation, but there is no explanation to offer. The anthropic principle tells us that "the universe needs to be the size and age it is in order for us to be here. . . . Why? Because the very elements of which our bodies are made were not present in the universe at the beginning."[5]

The elements, forces, metals, and minerals had to reach a perfect balance before life could be sustained. As Angela Tilby puts it, "The number

---

2. Tilby, *Soul*, 224–228.

3. Cited without attribution in Tilby, *Soul*, 223. For further discussion see Freeman Dyson, *Disturbing the Universe* (New York: Harper and Row, 1979), 251. See also the argument against the anthropic principle as a reliable scientific method: Ethan Siegel, "The Anthropic Principle Is What Scientists Use When They've Given Up on Science," *Forbes*, March 8, 2019, https://www.forbes.com/sites/startswitha-bang/2019/03/08/the-anthropic-principle-is-what-scientists-use-when-theyve-given-up-on-science/#721235e07724.

4. John Wheeler, as cited by Tilby, *Soul*, 229.

5. John Wheeler, as cited by Tilby, *Soul*, 216, 217.

of things which had to come out just right to produce us is enormous."[6] The weak anthropic principle argues that even though human beings are not the focus of the cosmos, it cannot be indifferent to our presence.[7] In other words, its intrinsic nature is supportive of "carbon-based life."[8]

Maybe, maybe not. As Polkinghorne points out, this version misses the wonder of a universe that developed the intricate biological and terrestrial processes necessary to sustain life on planet earth. If there were a plethora of life-sustaining ecosystems in our galaxy, or one that we could know about, our conclusion might be different. Instead, we enter a universe that is operating in a state of equilibrium between forces, energy, and matter in ways that allow us to be sustained.[9]

There are intricate interconnections between the space that we inhabit and the meaning that we seek. Although we may never unravel the mysteries, theology needs scientific perspectives as an enhancement of meaning and as a catalyst to the faith and awe that sustain religious life. Cultural studies also need an infusion of new perspectives to reassess goals and strategies.

Cultural Lessons from the Anthropic Principle

THE ANTHROPIC PRINCIPLE has been analyzed theologically as a proposition that can support or refute the argument for a universe that is designed by and involved with a creating God. Regardless of whether the anthropic principle is a reasonable scientific theory or reflects our own need to be centered in all conversations about reality, the following insights can enhance our reflective processes about race and identity on earth.

1. *Life is delicately balanced in the cosmos.* We could not exist otherwise. We live on a planet that could fly apart if the gravitational and electromagnetic forces were not perfectly balanced. Recent

---

6. Tilby, *Soul*, 222.

7. Ibid., 219.

8. Polkinghorne, *Science and Theology*, 37.

9. The term "anthropoi" is used in Polkinghorne's discussion of the principle in *Science and Theology*, 37.

RACE AND THE COSMOS

scientific information indicates that the balance may have shifted in favor of the anti-matter that is speeding the expansion of the universe. However, our needs are still being met.

But that is not the full story. If the universe requires our conscious knowing to be fulfilled, it requires not just some of us, or even the most powerful of us, but rather all of us, all of humankind in all of its diversity—gay, straight, female, able/disabled—to match the harmonies of an equally diverse cosmos. "There must be time and space . . . not only for the indicative mood of what is everlastingly the case, but also for the subjunctive and imperative moods of what might be, could be, and must be—the reign of God—against all the odds."[10] The diversity of cultures is necessary to the delicate balance of the universe. As it turns out, the order that we have imposed, the order that we sought, is not order at all.

2. *The universe is our mother.* Physicist David Bohm, who introduced us to the wholeness of the universe (implicate and explicate order), said, "Tribal cultures have said, 'The earth is our mother—we have to take care of the mother'; now people say, 'No that's not how it is. We've got to exploit the earth. . . . You can't count on your mother any more. You're on your own.'"[11]

    Current science positions the universe as the birthing place of all entities and thus a cosmic mother. New perspectives on the birthing aspects of the universe may also help to depict the life space as one that is intended to nurture. The intricate balances of chemicals and stardust, which must occur for life to appear, mimic the process of human birth. Science provides the images of the universe as initiating/siring and as an expanding womb, ready to sustain life. The birthing is mathematical, complex, and necessary. We are made in the image of a parent/creator who invites us into a cosmic belonging.

10. Toolan, "Praying," 6.
11. David Bohm, *On Dialogue*, ed. Lee Nichol (New York: Routledge, 1996), 91.

All of us need to belong somewhere. In an era when families are transient and fracturing, it has taken us too long to realize that nuclear (immediate) families lack an essential element necessary to foster and nurture its members. The isolation in these units can be complete and frightening.

When there is dysfunction, it can reach catastrophic proportions. Moreover, needs that surface within the microcosm of the nuclear family may go unmet. When I was living in Memphis, Tennessee, the city was shocked by the story of a nine-year-old boy who lived in the house with his dead mother for over a month.

When his mother died of cancer, the child covered her, went to school, shopped, cooked, and slept by her side. There was an extended family, but it was disconnected. The boy feared that the state would put him in foster care. To avoid that outcome, he tried to make it on his own. There was a time when his mother would have been missed in the neighborhood and help would have been only a few hours away.

It is not surprising that the move away from extended family coincides with the drive to create a massive and mobile labor force whose members will not balk at the transitory lifestyles that define our current culture. When nuclear family units veer into abuse or neglect, the support that could come from extended family relationships may be too distant to provide a safety net. When the elderly need care, there is often no one to nurture them as they nurtured others.

The Africana community often refers to Africa as the motherland and, while under the siege of slavery, it was not unusual for members of the African diaspora to treat each other as extended kin. Dr. Marcel Oyono tells me that in the Fon tribe in Cameroon, there are no words for extended kinship relationships like cousin or niece; instead, the words of immediate family are used— mother, brother, sister. This meant that a distant male relative was introduced to me as a "brother." These are rhetorical identifications that reflect an interconnected view of the life space.

We need the embrace of a Cosmic Mother. Whether or not she exists is not as important as our need for healing. For those under siege, it helps to know that we are supported and sustained by the cosmos that is our mother, and, as some theologians argue, maybe we are even loved by her.

3.   *Location affects perspective.* We can't view the whole universe or its component parts from where we stand. We are as embedded in the matrix of cosmic life as we are in daily events. Accordingly, we cannot know from personal and necessarily biased perspectives the needs of the "other" unless relationships remain intact.

The failure to admit our limited human perspectives leaves us open to the frightening potential of a repeat of past abuses. We don't know the explicit contours of radical evil. To pretend that we do means that we won't recognize reappearances in new configurations.

Once we are wedded to the image of evil as hooded night rider or global corporate invader, we are tricked by the desire for final answers. Every time we have projected outcomes, we have been surprised. Integration seemed to be a concept that had easily predictable consequences. People of all colors would live and work together in peace and harmony, racism would end, and opportunities would be available to all who wanted to participate in the "dream."

The reality is that racism has become the cunning social id. It is not dead, no matter what the collective ego says. A permanent underclass has developed among some ethnic groups, while the main American narrative ignores their reality. Native Americans are still forgotten and marginalized, beset by health problems and the psychic damage of decades of cultural annihilation. Yet the rhetoric of the casino successes of a few tribes obliterates this reality. African Americans occupy some of the highest governmental positions and command huge salaries as public figures, but the songs of success coming from the few have drowned out the bloody reality of gang violence, poverty, and mass incarceration.

From where we stand, we cannot see the whole picture. We don't know whether we are touching an elephant's tail or its trunk. If our information is coming from only one tactile source, then our description of the animal is going to be flawed. If our policies on race are developed from the limited perspectives that we have honed as we grasp the elephant's tail, they will serve only our own purposes. *We only know in part.* We need to repeat this mantra often, as it will keep us humble and alert.

4. *We live in incredible circumstances, with incredible responsibilities.* By the most enigmatic and specific of circumstances, the universe has all that we need to live and survive. To be living on a blue gem of a planet, breathing and sustained by the soil and the sea is a miracle. Whether this is an accident or a confirmation of faith depends on our perspective. The photographs taken from space stimulate the imagination. In the midst of barrenness and beauty, we look like a cosmic experiment. This may be as far from the truth as any other conclusion, but it's worth probing.

    Thus far, we have not found evidence of life elsewhere in our solar system. We don't know with certainty why the dinosaurs disappeared or why alligators or gorillas are not the more advanced species. For reasons that we do not know, we are the species responsible for responding with care to environmental issues and one another.

    From this perspective, respectful hosting of the mysteries that surround us and ethical engagement with the earth and its inhabitants seems to be the only responsible reply to the forces that induced/birthed/foreknew(?) our presence. This is the big picture. Suddenly, the rage engendered by issues of race and identity in North America seems manageable, a problem that can be approached on multiple levels. Certainly, justice must be done. The court battles and protests will invariably continue, but the human spirit must connect to a broader context. In the history of the universe, these temporary oppressors are insignificant. Praise for the nurture of the universe seems more appropriate to the human spirit, even in the face of atrocity and the interpositions of radical evil.

5. *We are here for a reason.* If, as the strong anthropic principle suggests, we are here for a reason, we ought to be about the task of finding out what it is and if it can be accomplished. We can assume from the diversity of the life space that the call to useful goals applies to all creatures.

The search for meaning should be approached with humility, for we are not the ultimate arbiters of the origins or fate of the universe. A deeper connection between scientific discourse and theology may lead to new questions that can guide our quest for fulfillment. The decisions that we make are inextricably connected to the ways in which we think. Those processes contribute to the search for meaning and may also be rooted in the quantum world.

Meaning and Consciousness

THE FIELD OF quantum physics has ignited a new approach to personhood, consciousness, and awareness that no one could have predicted. The first considerations of a physical premise for consciousness began in 1960, when Ninian Marshall opined that the brain could not account for "freedom" or human will. According to Marshall, experimentation indicated that the brain may be the primary locus of our awareness, but that this was only a starting point.[12] The amazing thing is that we have been able to study what we can't really understand. Until the advent of quantum studies of consciousness, we approached the idea through psychology and psychiatry.

Sigmund Freud recognized that a vast and unexplored inner world existed in humankind. He experimented with hypnosis, free association, and the study of dreams to unlock this area. Freud's approach was influenced by the Newtonian view of the world that assumed the ability to take apart a whole to examine its parts. According to Freud, one could descend from consciousness to unconsciousness and view the terrain. What he unearthed was a perspective on life that was predominately sexual. This approach would influence his therapeutic theories.

---

12. Zohar, *Quantum Self*, 79–80.

Carl Jung and Sigmund Freud were contemporaries. However, Jung took a different approach to human consciousness. Instead of dismantling consciousness to determine the contours of the unconscious, Jung proposed that the unconscious gave birth to the waking state. He concluded that we were born out of this state and return to it during sleep and upon death.

Like quantum events, the processes of the unconscious could only be ascertained indirectly and through assessment of probable correlations. One of Jung's important contributions was his discussion of the collective unconscious, or archetypes, that are identical in all human beings. As he wrote, "It is, to my mind, a fatal mistake to consider the human psyche as a merely personal affair and to explain it exclusively from a personal point of view."[13]

The collective unconscious is particularly relevant to a cultural study. It speaks to the ways in which groups of people respond to an ideology that has no roots in their experiential or genetic makeup. The positive manifestations of the collective unconscious are manifested as a repository of sedimented knowledge passed down from generation to generation. The collective unconsciousness is also being probed to determine its effects on physical processes. The Global Consciousness Project, started at Princeton University in 1998 and continuing today, questions whether "fields generated by individual consciousness could interact and combine, and ultimately have a global presence."[14]

Scientists are trying to determine whether consciousness can also affect reality. Computers at various locations around the globe track random data and quantum number stream variations. The experiment seeks information about the non-local interconnections of space, time, and mind, and the effects of emotion, attention, and inattention on the physical world. Initial reports indicate that consciousness may affect and be affected by objective reality. Their website reports data received prior to, during, and after global events like September 11, 2001 and the deaths of Princess Diana and John F. Kennedy Jr.[15]

---

13. Jung, *Psychology and Religion*, 16.

14. See The Global Consciousness Project, *Institute of Noetic Sciences*, http://noosphere.princeton.edu/homepage.html.

15. Ibid.

It is too soon to reach any conclusion as to the meaning of preliminary findings; however, The Global Consciousness Project statement is self-explanatory:

> We do not feel that our minds are isolated within our bodies. In truth, we experience the world with beautiful immediacy, we know our loved ones from afar, and we leap in thought to the stars. Research on anomalies of consciousness shows that we may have direct communication links with each other, and that intentions can have effects in the world despite physical barriers and separation.[16]

These connections and influences are not always positive. Walter Wink discussed the phenomena of collective possession.[17] He and Carl Jung point out the demonic and idolatrous aspects of the syndrome as exemplified in the Nazi atrocities, slavery, and ethnic cleansing.

We have attributed these effects to radical evil, which distances the phenomenon from our own actions. It seems that when we are possessed, we are unaware of it, as individuals and as a nation. It has been said that "the United States has never learned to listen to itself as if it were the enemy speaking."[18] Racism has also been described as a collective possession and evidence of the demonic "installed at the heart of national policy."[19] If racism is personal, collective, and part of the consciousness of the nation, perhaps, like quantum particles, it can't be nailed down or located in any particular person, group, or process. As a consequence, it may continue to erupt in unexpected forms until we turn our attention to its elements and use our collective energy to avert its effects.

---

16. Ibid.

17. Wink, *Unmasking the Powers*, 50–52.

18. Thomas Franck and Edward Weisband, *Word Politics: Verbal Strategy Among the Superpowers* (New York: Oxford University Press, 1971), 8, as quoted in Wink, *Unmasking the Powers*, 51. See also Morgan Marietta, *The Politics of Sacred Rhetoric: Absolutist Appeals and Political Persuasion* (Waco, TX: Baylor University Press, 2012).

19. Wink, *Unmasking the Powers*, 52.

What Women Can Mine from the New Discourses

MY MODEL FOR TESTING the theories in this book is "race," but I have no doubt that the lessons and rhetorical gifts of science may also have unique applications in the areas of gender and sexuality. The white feminist movement inverted the narrative of dominance by standing against the main patriarchal story. Black, Hispanic, Native American, and Asian women have taken a similar stance against the male hegemony within their own cultures. However, they have also resisted the homogenizing assumptions that white feminism imposed upon them.

Theologian Ellen Armour writes this about the intersecting boundaries of race and gender that continue to divide women: "Race constitutes an unexamined, unthematized, unthought ground of white feminist theory and theology."[20] Armour recognizes the premature nature of joint gender-equity projects while issues of race remain unsolved.

While each women's group resists male patriarchy, they also resist one another, carefully defining the differences and points of separation from the whole. Other ethnic groups and sexually marginalized people have borrowed the revolutionary tactics of the race/gender activist movements to amend and attach their own postscripts to the prevailing story.

But science and theology tell us that there is only one story. It is a human story and, yes, there are specific cultural and identity emphases, but we are connected in ways that won't allow the disjunctives of difference to define reality. If we decide that difference will be the defining discourse, we will have to attend more carefully to its complexities. On that issue, Armour writes,

> I am wary of monolithic treatments of "difference" as though any one difference were substitutable for another. . . . I suspect that each axis of difference (race, sexuality, class, etc.) follows a specific itinerary through particular fields of force that constitute and sustain

---

20. Ellen T. Armour, *Deconstruction, Feminist Theology, and the Problem of Difference: Subverting the Race/Gender Divide* (Chicago: University of Chicago Press, 1999), 2. See also Robin DiAngelo, *White Fragility: Why It's So Hard for White People to Talk about Racism* (Boston, MA: Beacon, 2018).

it. While these axes, their itineraries, and their histories intertwine with one another, they are not reducible to one another.[21]

While our unique experiences continue to divide us, we are reminded that, in the quantum world and in the cosmos, uniqueness does not foreclose holism and reunion.

A Return to Einstein

WE HAVE DISCUSSED the potential of meaning derived from scientific perspectives. Albert Einstein brought the quest into more mundane contexts. The man who changed science and our view of the life space urged those who seek meaning in life and in the creation to forego formulas, equations, and objectivity. In their place, he urged the pursuit of truth, goodness, and beauty. These three aesthetic and moral categories provide the framework to analyze the meaning of the preceding discussions of culture and the new physics and cosmology.

Truth

Those of us who have been influenced by the forces of deconstruction and the hermeneutics of critique hesitate to claim anything other than the potential for "truth." It is not that there is no truth, but that there is so much and so little, simultaneously. Truth, however it is defined, tends to be a rhetorical event. It is utterance that allows concepts and propositions to be embraced or refuted in private and public spaces. At the beginning of the twenty-first century, one wonders if there is any ascertainable truth about the stalled quest for justice and the potential for liberation theology.

The discussion thus far evinces several possibilities. If the languages of physics and cosmology are to be of any use to dominant and emerging cultures, those constituencies must bravely profess that religious, legislative/legal, and social discourses cannot, on their own, free us from the demonic forces of oppression in the world. The languages of

---

21. Ibid., 5.

liberation provided tools that began the process by deconstructing the myths of inferiority. They served well for this purpose, but they were never intended to provide the only resources for the journey to freedom.

This is another possible truth. The battle for liberation, wherever it is fought, inevitably wakens the beasts of systematic oppression. An awakened beast (no eschatological pun intended) is not safer than a sleeping ogre. Once the beast is awakened, only unlikely devices of the heart and mind can challenge it. In this regard, incongruity and absurdity are weapons that have vanquished formidable foes.

David and Goliath come to mind. In the biblical narrative (I Samuel 17), it is the sheer silliness and ostensible ineffectiveness of David's stone that surprises a victorious outcome. How else can a north star lead a slave woman from the deep south to Canada? How else can forgiveness and reconciliation be offered to participants of beer and human barbecue parties during South Africa's apartheid?[22]

The new physics and cosmology describe the life space in ways that disquiet dominance. The shifting perspectives offer opportunities to envision positive social outcomes for the body politic. The discourses of faith, law, sociology, and psychology need the addition of cosmic and quantum perspectives to achieve stated goals. The story of true liberation is seeded in tears and not upward mobility. In this post-King, post-Fannie Lou Hamer, post-Trayvon Martin, post-Nipsey Hussel, post-El Haj Malik El Shabazz (Malcom X) reality, the signposts toward moral flourishing and racial reconciliation are cosmic, technological, artistic, and social.

Goodness

Goodness is a first principle of the universe. God declares it on the first page of the story of creation. It is good to live in a universe that supports and nurtures us. In such an environment, we can think of goodness in terms of relationships, work, and God's good order. But we stumble

22. In a video shown at the Truth and Reconciliation Commission, white South Africans burned an African (after shooting him in the head) on a barbecue bonfire and stood around drinking while the corpse burned down to bones. Michael Ignatieff, "Something Happened," *The Guardian*, October 12, 2001, https://www.theguardian.com/theguardian/2001/oct/13/weekend7.weekend3.

when we come to the common good, for we can't determine what is common and what is good for all of us. Perhaps the translation of scientific findings into common discourse will help. It is good for the children of our nations to understand the nature of the universe. It is good to use the symbols and metaphors of science in cultural contexts. We will be amazed by the empowerment that results.

Ultimately, the good is realized when we reach agreement about a moral order that can guide our reconciliation efforts, but this requires our participation, vigilance, and repentance. We must repent because even when we courted evil, we knew what was good; even when we eschewed virtue, we knew its embrace. If indeed there is a moral arc to the universe, then we will be held accountable if we fail to bend in its direction.

Beauty

In the black community, mothers and "other mothers" used to say, "Beauty is as beauty does." What is beautiful is also beneficial to the community. What is beautiful may have nothing to do with the curl in your hair or the swirl of your skirt. Those who truly know the meaning of the term revere some of the most ordinary folks as beautiful.

In the scientific realm, there is beauty in symmetry, but symmetry tends to obviate the emergence of diversity. If beauty is in the eye of the beholder, we are blinded by cultural presumptions. Dying to be thin, praying to be free, we seek beauty in places where it cannot be found. There is beauty in truth-telling—speaking truth to power, there is beauty in the care of those who cannot care for themselves.

Finally, there is beauty in a realization that divine and human realities exceed our expectations and descriptions. The life that we have been granted is beautiful in every respect, notwithstanding its suffering. Racism, oppression, and domination are anomalies in a universe that was proclaimed good by the One who declares beauty, truth, and goodness to be normative and intrinsic aspects of the life space.

Summary

OUR SEARCH FOR MEANING reveals eleven dimensions (or more) in a life space where there are no centers or margins, no need to struggle or resist self-proclaimed hegemonies. In fact, there may actually be space to explore the human task. Even though connections to a holistic and vibrantly alive and reactive universe will not end the struggle for justice, it might place those struggles in perspective. The universe is diverse and whole. Perhaps the path to freedom and the meaning of our lives is outlined in the stars, and perhaps increasing diversity will ensure the freedom that has been the subject of our waking dreams.

:::

Conclusion:
When We Consider How Our Lives Are Spent

I still believe in hope, not hate.
I still believe in courage, not cowardice.
I still believe in the values that Medgar Evers
[and others] lived and died for. As my 85th
birthday nears, I am more determined than
ever to see that those values persist.
                                    —Myrlie Evers

Become your ancestor's wildest dream.
                                    —Ava DuVernay

YRLIE EVERS, WIDOW of slain civil rights activist Medgar Evers (1925–1963), spent Dr. Martin Luther King, Jr., Day 2018 wiping away tears during the opening of the Mississippi Civil Rights Museum. She said that she was "weeping for a nation where racism, once believed dead, has begun to bud and bloom."[1]

---

1. "Myrlie Evers: I Weep for a Nation Where Racism Has Begun to Bloom Again,"

For the last few decades, we have glared steadily at issues of racism and ethnicity. We applied our best solutions with relentless diligence, only to watch the issues return with appalling virulence and resilience. Now, another generation marches with the same intent to wrest justice from the powers and principalities that hold us captive. But, they may not fare much better than we did unless they shift their gaze, intention, and energy.

It is time to shift the focus of activism from resistance to the improvisational creation of the community-called-beloved. "Improvisation creates opportunities for laughter, community formation, and sharing, even while we continue the work of justice."[2]

Afrofuturism also offers an opportunity to bring this vision into view. Afrofuturism is a philosophical, artistic, and sci-fi reclamation of the past, present, and cosmic future of African diasporan people. "Afrofuturism transforms trauma, the erasure of the black past, and bleak prospects for the future into powerful displays of creative agency."[3]

When we consider how our lives are lived through a cosmological lens, we must include our planetary as well as social contexts. The discourses of physics and cosmology urge us to blink, to rebuild our health, communities, and value systems. I urge the next generation to attend to their trauma and their healing as a first step toward full agency. We prioritize our personal wellbeing so that we can survive to connect with others. Solutions to the creation of an egalitarian society may always be just beyond our reach because racism and anti-black beliefs include spiritual malignancies that are not easily displaced.

However, as we continue the struggle for justice, the universe invites us toward expanded options. We can incorporate the wonder of science

Clarionledger.com, January 19, 2018.

2. Barbara A. Holmes, "Still on the Journey: Moral Witness, Imagination, and Improvisation in Public Life," in *Ethics that Matters: African, Caribbean, and African American Sources,* eds. Marcia Y. Riggs and James Samuel Logan (Minneapolis: Fortress, 2012), 237.

3. Josh Jones, "Watch a 5-Part Animated Primer on Afrofuturism, the Black Sci-Fi Phenomenon Inspired by Sun Ra," *Open Culture*, March 9, 2017, https://www.openculture.com/2017/03/animated-primer-on-afrofuturism.html. See also Alisha B. Wormsley, "There Are Black People in the Future," https://alishabwormsley.com/new-page-1.

in our liturgy, prayers, and politics. We can strengthen and challenge theological precepts by including information about the intricacies of the cosmos in our everyday lives. We can respect the differences of light and dark as alternating and equal powers in the universe and we can become our ancestor's wildest dream.[4]

Finally, we can embrace the expectancy and potential of the quantum world and find our place of belonging within its dynamic uncertainties. Perhaps we will find pathways toward one another when we consider how our lives are spent within a complex cosmos. However, we will not wrest an egalitarian order from the persisting chaos with swords drawn or in fitful daydreams. Instead, we commit ourselves to "staying woke" and doing the difficult work of knowing self, others, and the universe as integral parts of a cosmic order that announces its Author, our liberation, and the human potential for transcendence in every star and galaxy.[5]

---

4. Ava DuVernay, "Become your ancestor's wildest dream," *Twitter*, August 5, 2017, 9:33 a.m., https://twitter.com/ava/status/893872487716585475.

5. The title of this Conclusion is a reference to John Milton's poem, "When I Consider How My Light Is Spent," (1652–1655), https://poets.org/poem/when-i-consider-how-my-light-spent.

::::

Bibliography

Science

Aspinwall, Paul S., Brian R. Greene, and David R. Morrison. "Multiple Mirror Manifolds and Topology Change in String Theory." *Physics Letters* B 303 (3–4): 249–259, April 1993.

Barrow, John D., and Frank J. Tipler. *The Anthropic Cosmological Principle.* New York: Oxford University Press, 1986.

Bartusiak, Marcia. *The Day We Found the Universe.* New York: Vintage, 2009.

————. *Through a Universe Darkly: A Cosmic Tale of Ancient Ethers, Dark Matter, and the Fate of the Universe.* New York: Avon, 1993.

Bernstein, Jeremy. "I Am This Whole World: Erwin Schrödinger." In *Project Physics Reader* 5. New York: Holt, Rinehart and Winston, 1968–1969.

Bohm, David. *Wholeness and the Implicate Order.* New York: Routledge, 1996.

Bohm, David, and Basil. J. Hiley. *The Undivided Universe: An Ontological Interpretation of Quantum Theory.* New York: Routledge, 1993.

Davies, Paul. *Cosmic Jackpot: Why Our Universe Is Just Right for Life.* New York: Houghton Mifflin, 2007.

————. *God and the New Physics.* New York: Simon & Schuster, 1983.

deGrasse Tyson, Neil. *Death by Black Hole: And Other Cosmic Quandaries*. New York: W. W. Norton, 2007.

Dembski, William A. *The Design Revolution: Answering the Toughest Questions about Intelligent Design*. Downers Grove, IL: InterVarsity, 2004.

Doyle, Laurence R., and Edward W. Frank. "Astronomy of Africa." In *Encyclopaedia of the History of Science, Technology, and Medicine in Non-Western Cultures*, edited by Helaine Selin. Norwell, MA: Kluwer Academic Publishers, 1997.

Dyson, Freeman J. *Infinite in All Directions*. New York: Harper, 1988.

Einstein, Albert. *The World as I See It*. New York: Carol Publishing, 1998.

Freese, Katherine. *The Cosmic Cocktail: Three Parts Dark Matter*. Princeton: Princeton University Press, 2014.

Glanz, James. "Evidence of Mystery Particles Stirring Excitement and Doubt." *New York Times* (February 19, 2000).

Greene, Brian. *The Elegant Universe: Superstrings, Hidden Dimensions, and the Quest for the Ultimate Theory*. New York: Vintage, 1999.

———. *The Fabric of the Cosmos: Space, Time, and the Texture of Reality*. New York: Alfred A. Knopf, 2004.

Gonzalez, Guillermo, and Jay W. Richards. *The Privileged Planet: How Our Place in the Cosmos Is Designed for Discovery*. Washington, DC: Regnery, 2004.

Gould, Roy R. *Universe in Creation: A New Understanding of the Big Bang and the Emergence of Life*. Cambridge, MA: Harvard University Press, 2018.

Harding, Sandra, ed. *The "Racial" Economy of Science: Toward a Democratic Future*. Bloomington, IN: Indiana University Press, 1993.

Hawking, Stephen. *Brief Answers to the Big Questions*. New York: Bantam, 2018.

Heisenberg, Werner. *The Physicist's Conception of Nature,* translated by Arnold J. Pomerans. New York: Harcourt Brace, 1958.

———. "Truth Dwells in the Deeps." In *Quantum Questions: Mystical Writings of the World's Greatest Physicists,* edited by Ken Wilber, 33–39. Boston: Shambhala, 2001.

Herbert, Nick. *Quantum Reality: Beyond the New Physics.* New York: Anchor, 1985.

Hetherington, Norriss S. *Cosmology: Historical, Literary, Philosophical, Religious, and Scientific Perspectives.* New York: Garland, 1993.

Kaku, Michio. *Hyperspace: A Scientific Odyssey Through Parallel Universes, Time Warps, and the 10th Dimension.* New York: Anchor, 1995.

————. *Physics of the Future: How Science Will Shape Human Destiny and Our Daily Lives by the Year 2100.* New York: Doubleday, 2011.

————. *Visions: How Science Will Revolutionize the 21st Century.* New York: Anchor, 1998.

Kaku, Michio, and Jennifer Thompson. *Beyond Einstein: The Cosmic Quest for the Theory of the Universe.* New York: Anchor, 1995.

Kuhn, Thomas S. *The Structure of Scientific Revolutions: 50th Anniversary Edition.* Chicago: University of Chicago Press, 2012.

Lemonick, Michael D. "Einstein's Repulsive Idea." *Time* (April 16, 2001): 58.

Morris, Richard. *The Edges of Science: Crossing the Boundary from Physics to Metaphysics.* New York: Prentice Hall, 1990.

Murdoch, Dugald. *Niels Bohr's Philosophy of Physics.* Cambridge, England: Cambridge University Press, 1987.

Pagels, Heinz R. *The Cosmic Code: Quantum Physics as the Language of Nature.* New York: Simon & Schuster, 1982.

Parker, Barry. *Einstein's Dream: The Search for a Unified Theory of the Universe.* New York: Perseus, 1986.

Peat, F. David. *Infinite Potential: The Life and Times of David Bohm.* Reading, MA: Addison Wesley, 1997.

————. *Lighting the Seventh Fire: The Spiritual Ways, Healing, and Science of the Native American.* New York: Citadel, 1994.

Planck, Max. *Where Is Science Going?* New York: Norton, 1932.

Polkinghorne, John. *The Polkinghorne Reader: Science, Faith and the Search for Meaning.* London: Society for Promoting Christian Knowledge, 2010.

————. *Science and Theology: An Introduction.* Minneapolis: Fortress, 1998.

Pond, Dale. "It Really Is a Musical Universe!" *Sympathetic Vibratory Physics* (November 1999), https://www.svpvril.com/musicuni.html.

Popp, Fritz-Albert, K. H. Li, W. P. Mei, M. Galle, and R. Neurohr. "Physical Aspects of Biophotons." *Experientia* 44 (1988): 576–585.

Rubin, Vera C. *Bright Galaxies, Dark Matters.* New York: Springer-Verlag, 1996.

————. "Dark Matter in the Universe." *Scientific American* 280, no. 3 (March 1999): 2.

Sagan, Carl. *The Demon-Haunted World: Science as a Candle in the Dark*. New York: Ballantine, 1996.

Smith, Nigel, and Neil Spooner. "The Search for Dark Matter." *Physics World* 13, no. 1 (January 2000): 1–8.

Stegall, William. "A Guide to A. N. Whitehead's *Understanding of God and the Universe*." In *Creative Transformation,* Center for Process Studies (Spring 1995).

Swimme, Brian. *The Hidden Heart of the Cosmos: Humanity and the New Story*. Maryknoll, NY: Orbis, 1996.

Swimme, Brian, and Thomas Berry. *The Universe Story*. San Francisco: HarperSanFrancisco, 1992.

Taylor, Barbara Brown. *The Luminous Web: Essays on Science and Religion*. Cambridge, MA: Cowley, 2000.

Tilby, Angela. *Soul: God, Self, and the New Cosmology*. New York: Doubleday, 1993.

Tucker, Wallace, and Karen Tucker. *The Dark Matter: Contemporary Science's Quest for the Mass Hidden in Our Universe*. New York: William Morrow, 1988.

Weizenbaum, Joseph. *Computer Power and Human Reason: From Judgment to Calculation*. San Francisco: Freeman, 1976.

Wilber, Ken. *Quantum Questions: Mystical Writings of the World's Greatest Physicists*. Boston: Shambhala, 2001.

Wolf, Fred Alan. *Taking the Quantum Leap: The New Physics for Non-Scientists*. New York: Harper & Row, 1989.

Zohar, Danah. *The Quantum Self: Human Nature and Consciousness Defined by the New Physics*. New York: William Morrow, 1990.

Zukav, Gary. *The Dancing Wu Li Masters: An Overview of the New Physics*. New York: Bantam, 1979.

Culture

Abrams, Nancy Ellen, and Joel R. Primack. "Cosmology and 21st-Century Culture." *Science* 293, no. 5536 (September 7, 2001): 1769–1770.

Anderson, Victor. *Beyond Ontological Blackness: An Essay on African American Religious and Cultural Criticism*. New York: Bloomsbury, 2016.

Ani, Marimba. *Yurugu: An African-Centered Critique of European Cultural Thought and Behavior.* Trenton, NJ: Africa World Press, 1994.

Armour, Ellen T. *Deconstruction, Feminist Theology, and the Problem of Difference: Subverting the Race/Gender Divide.* Chicago: University of Chicago Press, 1999.

Bastien, Betty. "Coming to Know: Research Methodology." Native Research and Scholarship Symposium, Orcas Island, Washington, July 21, 1996.

Berman, Harold J. "Law and Love." In *Faith and Order: The Reconciliation of Law and Religion.* Atlanta: Scholars Press, 1993.

Brace, C. Loring. Foreword to *Man's Most Dangerous Myth: The Fallacy of Race,* by Ashley Montagu. 6th ed. Walnut Creek, CA: AltaMira, 1997.

Christensen, Rosemary Ackley. "A Frame for the Native Intellect: Celebrated, Solicited, and Revealed." Native Research and Scholarship Symposium, Orcas Island, Washington, July 21–22, 1996.

Cone, James H. *A Black Theology of Liberation.* Maryknoll, NY: Orbis, 2010.

———. *God of the Oppressed.* Maryknoll, NY: Orbis, 2003.

———. *Risks of Faith: The Emergence of a Black Theology of Liberation 1968–1998.* Boston: Beacon, 1999.

Conti, Gary J. "Research in the Tribal Community: Two Research Paradigms." Native Research and Scholarship Symposium, Orcas Island, Washington, July 21–22, 1996.

Cook, Anthony E. *The Least of These: Race, Law, and Religion in American Culture.* New York: Routledge, 1997.

Crosley, Reginald. *The Vodou Quantum Leap: Alternate Realities, Power, and Mysticism.* München, Germany: Theion Publishing, 2014.

Delgado, Richard. *When Equality Ends: Stories About Race and Resistance.* Boulder, CO: Westview, 1999.

Delgado, Richard, and Jean Stefancic, eds. *Critical Race Theory: The Cutting Edge.* Temple University Press, 2013.

Deloria, Vine, Jr. *Custer Died for Your Sins.* New York: Macmillan, 1969.

————. *For This Land: Writings on Religion in America*. New York: Routledge, 1999.

————. *Red Earth, White Lies: North Americans and the Myth of Scientific Fact*. New York: Scribner, 1995.

————. *The World We Used to Live In: Remembering the Powers of the Medicine Men*. Golden, CO: Fulcrum, 2006.

Dyer, Richard. *White*. New York: Routledge, 1997 and *White: Twentieth Anniversary Edition*. New York: Routledge, 2017.

Dyson, Michael Eric. *I May Not Get There with You: The True Martin Luther King Jr*. New York: Free Press, 2000.

Earl, Riggins R., Jr. *Dark Symbols, Obscure Signs: God, Self, and Community in the Slave Mind*. Maryknoll, NY: Orbis, 1993.

Ehrlich, Paul R., and S. Shirley Feldman. *The Race Bomb: Skin Color, Prejudice, and Intelligence*. New York: Quadrangle, 1977.

Ellison, Ralph. *Shadow and Act*. New York: Vintage, 1972.

Farley, Edward. *Deep Symbols: Their Postmodern Effacement and Reclamation*. Harrisburg, PA: Trinity Press International, 1996.

Gould, Stephen Jay. "American Polygeny and Craniometry Before Darwin." In *The "Racial" Economy of Science: Toward a Democratic Future*, edited by Sandra Harding, 84–115. Bloomington, IN: Indiana University Press, 1993.

Gresson, Aaron David, III. *The Recovery of Race in America*. Minneapolis: University of Minnesota Press, 1995.

Hamilton, Virginia, and Leo and Diane Dillon. *The People Could Fly: American Black Folktales*. New York: Alfred A. Knopf, 1993.

Highwater, Jamake. *The Primal Mind: Vision and Reality in Indian America*. New York: Harper & Row, 1981.

Howard, Michael C., and Patrick C. McKim. *Contemporary Cultural Anthropology*. Boston: Little, Brown, 1983.

Inchausti, Robert. *Spitwad Sutras: Classroom Teaching as Sublime Vocation*. Westport, CT: Bergin & Garvey, 1993.

Jernigan, Valarie Blue Bird. "Community-Based Participatory Research with Native American Communities: The Chronic Disease Self-Management Program." *Health Promotion Practice* 11, no. 6 (November 2010): 888–899.

Jung, Carl G. *Psychology and Religion.* New Haven: Yale University Press, 1938, 1966.

Kanpol, Barry, and Peter McLaren, eds. *Critical Multiculturalism: Uncommon Voices in a Common Struggle.* Westport, CT: Bergin & Garvey, 1995.

Kwok, Pui-Lan. *Introducing Asian Feminist Theology.* Cleveland: Pilgrim, 2000.

Liddell, Janice. *Imani and the Flying Africans.* New York: Africa World Press, 1994.

Lynch, B. M., and L. H. Robbins. "Namoratunga: The First Archaeoastronomical Evidence in Sub-Saharan Africa." *Science* 200, no. 4343 (June 1978): 766–768.

Martin, Clarice J. "Somebody Done Hoodoo'd the Hoodoo Man: Language, Power, Resistance, and the Effective History of Pauline Texts in American Slavery." *Semeia* 83/84 (1998): 203–233.

Martínez, David. *Life of the Indigenous Mind: Vine Deloria Jr. and the Birth of the Red Power Movement.* Lincoln, NE: University of Nebraska Press; Philadelphia: American Philosophical Society, 2019.

McKenna, Megan, and Tony Cowan. *Keepers of the Story.* Maryknoll, NY: Orbis, 1997.

Morgan, Stacy I. "Dust Tracks Untrampled by the Dinosaur of History: The Ibo's Landing and Flying Africans Narratives as Mythic Counter-Memory." *Sycamore: A Journal of American Culture* 1.1 (Spring 1997).

Peacock, Thomas D. "Issues in American Indian Research: The Perspective of a Reservation Indian." Native Research and Scholarship Symposium, Orcas Island, Washington, July 21–22, 1996.

Pieris, Aloysius. *An Asian Theology of Liberation.* Maryknoll, NY: Orbis, 1988.

Rigby, Cynthia L. "Someone to Blame, Someone to Trust: Divine Power and the Self-Recovery of the Oppressed." In *Power, Powerlessness, and the Divine: New Inquiries in Bible and Theology,* edited by Cynthia L. Rigby, 79–102. Atlanta: Scholars Press, 1997.

Riggs, Marcia Y. *Awake, Arise, and Act: A Womanist Call for Black Liberation.* Cleveland: Pilgrim, 1994.

Robinson, Randall. *The Debt: What America Owes to Blacks.* New York: Penguin, 2000.

Scranton, Laird. *The Science of the Dogon: Decoding the African Mystery Tradition.* Rochester, VT: Inner Traditions, 2006.

Smith, Theophus H. *Conjuring Culture: Biblical Formations of Black America.* New York: Oxford University Press, 1994.

Somé, Malidoma Patrice. *Of Water and the Spirit: Ritual, Magic, and Initiation in the Life of an African Shaman.* New York: Penguin, 1994.

Swimme, Brian. "The Resurgence of Cosmic Storytellers." *The NAMTA Journal* 38, no. 1 (Winter 2013): 165–171.

Tandon, R. "Participatory Research in the Empowerment of People." *Convergence* 14, no. 3 (1981): 20–29.

Thomas, Linda E. "Womanist Theology, Epistemology, and a New Anthropological Paradigm." *Cross Currents* 48, no. 4 (Summer 1998): 4.

Toolan, David S. "Praying in a Post-Einsteinian Universe." *Cross Currents* 46, no. 4 (Winter 1996–1997): 437–470.

Tuan, Yi-Fu. *Passing Strange and Wonderful: Aesthetics, Nature, and Culture.* New York: Kodansha International, 1995.

Tucker, William H. *The Science and Politics of Racial Research.* Champaign, IL: University of Illinois Press, 1993.

West, Cornel. *Race Matters.* New York: Vintage, 1994.

White, Charles. *An Account of the Regular Gradation in Man and in Different Animals and Vegetables; and from the Former to the Latter.* London: C. Dilly, 1799.

Young, Iris Marion. "Five Faces of Oppression." In *Multiculturalism from the Margins: Non-Dominant Voices on Difference and Diversity,* edited by Dean A. Harris, 65–86. Westport, CT: Bergin & Garvey, 1995.

Theology

Barash, David. *Beloved Enemies: Our Need for Opponents.* Amherst, NY: Prometheus, 1994.

Barber, Michael. "The Ethics Behind the Absence of Ethics in Alfred Schütz's Thought." *Human Studies: A Journal for Philosophy and the Social Sciences* 14 (July 1991): 129–140.

Barbour, Ian G. *Religion in an Age of Science: The Gifford Lectures, Vol. 1.* San Francisco: HarperSanFrancisco, 1990.

————. *When Science Meets Religion: Enemies, Strangers, or Partners?* New York: HarperOne, 2000.

Boff, Leonardo, and Clodovis Boff. *Introducing Liberation Theology.* Maryknoll, NY: Orbis, 1987.

Bounds, Elizabeth M. "Conflicting Harmonies: Michael Walzer's Vision of Community." *Journal of Religious Ethics* 22, no. 2 (Fall 1994): 355–374.

Brueggemann, Walter E. *Journey to the Common Good.* Louisville, KY: Westminster John Knox, 2010.

————. *Threat of Life: Sermons on Pain, Power, and Weakness.* Minneapolis: Fortress, 1996.

Cone, James. *A Black Theology of Liberation.* Maryknoll, NY: Orbis, 2010.

Davies, Paul. "Is the Universe Absurd?" In *Science and Theology: The New Consonance,* edited by Ted Peters, 65–76. Boulder, CO: Westview, 1998.

Deloria, Vine, Jr. *God Is Red: A Native View of Religion.* 30th Anniversary Edition. Golden, CO: Fulcrum, 2003.

Haught, John F. *The New Cosmic Story: Inside Our Awakening Universe.* New Haven: Yale University Press, 2017.

————. *Science and Religion: From Conflict to Conversation.* Mahwah, NJ: Paulist, 1995.

Holmes, Barbara A. *Liberation and the Cosmos: Conversations with the Elders.* Minneapolis: Fortress, 2008.

Hood, Robert. *Must God Remain Greek? Afro Cultures and God-Talk.* Minneapolis: Fortress, 1990.

Hopkins, Dwight N. *Being Human: Race, Culture, and Religion.* Minneapolis: Augsburg Fortress, 2005.

Hopkins, Dwight N., and George Cummings, eds. *Cut Loose Your Stammering Tongue: Black Theology in the Slave Narratives.* Maryknoll, NY: Orbis, 1991.

Isasi-Díaz, Ada María. *Mujerista Theology.* Maryknoll, NY: Orbis, 1996.

Jammer, Max. *Einstein and Religion: Physics and Theology.* Princeton: Princeton University Press, 1999.

Levine, Daniel H. "The Future of Liberation Theology." *Journal of the International Institute* 2, no. 2 (Winter 1995): 1–3.

Mesle, C. Robert. *Process Theology: A Basic Introduction.* St. Louis: Chalice, 1993.

Murphy, Nancey, and George F. R. Ellis. *On the Moral Nature of the Universe: Theology, Cosmology, and Ethics.* Minneapolis: Fortress, 1996.

Oduyoye, Mercy Amba. "Reflections from a Third World Woman's Perspective: Women's Experience and Liberation Theologies." In *Feminist Theology from the Third World: A Reader,* edited by Ursula King, 23–34. Maryknoll, NY: Orbis, 1994.

O'Murchu, Diarmuid. *In the Beginning was the Spirit: Science, Religion, and Indigenous Spirituality.* Maryknoll, NY: Orbis, 2012.

———. *Quantum Theology: Spiritual Implications of the New Physics.* New York: Crossroad, 2000.

Palmer, Parker. "Spiritual Formation and Social Change." In *Fugitive Faith: Interviews by Benjamin Webb,* 56–67. Maryknoll, NY: Orbis, 1998.

Pedraja, Luis G. *Jesus Is My Uncle: Christology from a Hispanic Perspective.* Nashville: Abingdon, 1999.

Peters, Ted. *God—The World's Future: Systematic Theology for a New Era.* Minneapolis: Fortress, 2000.

———, ed. *Science and Theology: The New Consonance.* Boulder, CO: Westview, 1998.

Rahner, Karl. *Foundations of Christian Faith.* New York: Seabury, 1978.

Sharpe, Kevin. *Sleuthing the Divine: The Nexus of Science and Spirit.* Minneapolis: Fortress, 2000.

Solomon, Jack. *The Signs of Our Time: The Secret Meanings of Everyday Life.* New York: Harper & Row, 1988.

Tanner, Kathryn. *The Politics of God: Christian Theologies and Social Justice.* Minneapolis: Augsburg Fortress, 1992.

Thurman, Howard. *Meditations of the Heart.* New York: Harper & Row, 1953.

Wells, Albert N. *The Christian Message in a Scientific Age.* Richmond, VA: John Knox, 1962.

West, Cornel. *The Cornel West Reader.* New York: Basic Civitas, 1999.

Wink, Walter. *Engaging the Powers: Discernment and Resistance in a World of Domination.* Minneapolis: Fortress, 1992.

——— . *Naming the Powers: The Language of Power in the New Testament.* Minneapolis: Fortress, 1984.

——— . *The Powers That Be: Theology for a New Millennium.* Minneapolis: Fortress, 1998.

——— . *Unmasking the Powers: The Invisible Forces That Determine Human Existence.* Minneapolis: Fortress, 1986.

——— . *When the Powers Fall: Reconciliation in the Healing of Nations.* Minneapolis: Fortress, 1998.

Wolf, Fred Alan. *The Spiritual Universe: One Physicist's Vision of Spirit, Soul, Matter, and Self.* Portsmouth, NH: Moment Point Press, 1999.

Young, Henry James. *Hope in Process: A Theology of Social Pluralism.* Minneapolis: Fortress, 1990.

Zaleski, Carol. "In Defense of Immortality." *First Things* 105 (August–September 2000): 36–42.

Rhetoric

Bakhtin, M. M. *The Dialogic Imagination: Four Essays,* edited and translated by Michael Holquist. Austin: University of Texas Press, 1981.

Bohm, David. *On Dialogue,* edited by Lee Nichol. New York: Routledge, 1996.

du Preez, Peter. "Reason Which Cannot Be Reasoned With: What Is Public Debate and How Does It Change?" In *Empirical Logic and Public Debate: Essays in Honour of Else M. Barth,* edited by Erick C. W. Krabbe, Renee Jose Dalitz, and Pier A. Smit, 211–226. Atlanta: Rodopi, 1993.

Edgar, Amanda Nell, and Andre E. Johnson. *The Struggle over Black Lives Matter and All Lives Matter.* Lanham, MD: Lexington, 2018.

Gregory, Bruce. *Inventing Reality: Physics as Language.* New York: John Wiley & Sons, 1988.

Holmes, Barbara A., and the Honorable Susan Holmes Winfield. "King, the Constitution, and the Courts: Remaining Awake Through a Great Revolution." In *The Legacy of Martin Luther King, Jr.: The Boundaries of Law, Politics, and Religion*, edited by Lewis V. Baldwin. Notre Dame, IN: University of Notre Dame Press, 2002.

Johnson, Barbara. *A World of Difference*. Baltimore: Johns Hopkins University Press, 1987.

Kennedy, Tammie M., Joyce Irene Middleton, and Krista Ratcliffe, eds. *Rhetorics of Whiteness: Postracial Hauntings in Popular Culture, Social Media, and Education*. Carbondale, IL: Southern Illinois University Press, 2017.

Ore, Ersula J. *Lynching: Violence, Rhetoric, and American Identity*. Jackson, MS: University Press of Mississippi, 2019.

Robbins, Vernon K. "The Present and Future of Rhetorical Analysis." In *The Rhetorical Analysis of Scripture: Essays from the 1995 London Conference*, edited by Stanley E. Porter and Thomas H. Olbricht. Sheffield, England: Sheffield Academic Press, 1997.

Stepan, Nancy Leys. "Race and Gender: The Role of Analogy in Science." In *The "Racial" Economy of Science: Toward a Democratic Future*, edited by Sandra Harding, 359–376. Bloomington, IN: Indiana University Press, 1993.

Stepan, Nancy Leys, and Sander L. Gilman. "Appropriating the Idioms of Science: The Rejection of Scientific Racism." In *The "Racial" Economy of Science: Toward a Democratic Future*, edited by Sandra Harding, 170–200. Bloomington, IN: Indiana University Press, 1993.

Washington, James M., ed. *A Testimony of Hope: The Essential Writings and Speeches of Martin Luther King, Jr.* San Francisco: HarperCollins, 1986.

Philosophy

Chamcham, Khalil, Joseph Silk, John D. Barrow, and Simon Saunders, eds. *The Philosophy of Cosmology*. Cambridge, England: Cambridge University Press, 2017.

Corbett, Jim. *Goatwalking: A Guide to Wildland Living, a Quest for the Peaceable Kingdom*. New York: Viking, 1991.

Derrida, Jacques. "Some Statements and Truisms about Neologisms, Newisms, Postisms, Parasitisms, and other Small Seismisms." In *The States* of *"Theory": History, Art, and Critical Discourse,* edited by David Carroll, 63–94. New York: Columbia University Press, 1990.

Morrison, Toni. *Playing in the Dark: Whiteness and the Literary Imagination.* New York: Vintage, 1993.

Nesteruk, Alexei V. *The Sense of the Universe: Philosophical Explication of Theological Commitment in Modern Cosmology.* Minneapolis: Fortress, 2015.

Rasmussen, Larry L. *Earth Community, Earth Ethics.* Maryknoll, NY: Orbis, 1996.

Richo, David. *Everything Ablaze: Meditations on the Mystical Vision of Teilhard de Chardin.* New York: Paulist, 2017.

Schütz, Alfred. "Don Quixote and the Problem of Reality." In *Collected Papers 2: Studies in Social Theory,* edited by Arvid Brodersen, 135–158. The Hague: Martinus Nijhoff, 1964.

Schütz, Alfred, and Thomas Luckmann. *The Structures of the Life-World,* translated by Richard M. Zaner and H. Tristram Engelhardt, Jr. Evanston, IL: Northwestern University Press, 1973.

Wilshire, Bruce. *The Primal Roots of American Philosophy: Pragmatism, Phenomenology, and Native American Thought.* University Park, PA: Pennsylvania State University Press, 2000.

Literature

Baldwin, James. *No Name in the Street.* New York: Dial, 1972.

Bambara, Toni Cade. *The Sea Birds Are Still Alive.* New York: Random House, 1974.

Big Eagle, Duane. "My Grandfather Was a Quantum Physicist." In *Songs from This Earth on Turtle's Back: Contemporary American Indian Poetry,* edited by Joseph Bruchac, 22. Greenfield Center, NY: Greenfield Review Press, 1983.

Coates, Ta-Nehisi. *Between the World and Me.* New York: Spiegel & Grau, 2015.

Cortázar, Julio. *Hopscotch: A Novel,* translated by Gregory Rabassa. New York: Random House, 1995.

Lewis, C. S. *Perelandra.* New York: Macmillan, 1946.

Lorde, Audre. "Who Said It Was Simple." In *Chosen Poems: Old and New*, 49–50. New York: W. W. Norton, 1982.

Morrison, Toni. *Song of Solomon.* New York: Vintage, 2004.

Young, Al. *African American Literature: A Brief Introduction and Anthology.* New York: HarperCollins, 1996.

Rev. Dr. Barbara A. Holmes is a spiritual teacher and writer who focuses on African American spirituality, mysticism, cosmology, and culture. A faculty member of the Center for Action and Contemplation's Living School, she is President Emerita of United Theological Seminary of the Twin Cities and served as Vice President of Academic Affairs and Dean of Memphis Theological Seminary. Dr. Holmes was called to ministry while working as a lawyer who specialized in civil litigation, corporate, and appellate practice. She was ordained in the Latter Rain Apostolic Holiness Church in Dallas, Texas. Dr. Holmes has worked with homeless missions, HIV/AIDS support groups, and international ministries in Kenya and Japan. The author of five books and numerous articles, her publications include *Liberation and the Cosmos: Conversations with the Elders* and *Joy Unspeakable: Contemplative Practices of the Black Church.* Learn more about Dr. Holmes at drbarbaraholmes.com.